The Best of PEOPLE The First Decade

THE **BEST** OF

People weekly

THE·FIRST·DECADE

BY THE EDITORS
OF PEOPLE WEEKLY

EDITOR
CRANSTON JONES

ART DIRECTOR
GREGORY B. LEEDS

PICTURE EDITOR
MARY DUNN

ASSOCIATE EDITORS
RICHARD C. LEMON
ROGER R. WOLMUTH

RESEARCHERS
MARTHA K. BABCOCK
LEE POWELL

**ASSISTANT
PICTURE EDITOR**
JUDITH LAUFER

COPY EDITORS
MARTIN GREENFIELD
MURIEL C. ROSENBLUM

TYPESETTER
CARMINE A. MODE

**ASSISTANT
ART DIRECTOR**
BARBARA EGAN

Valuable assistance was given by the following:
managing editor Patricia Ryan; editors Jim Calio, Jim Jerome
and Irene Neves; indexer Dianne Cyrus; Jean L. Reynolds; Hillary Weiss,
Time Inc. Picture Collection; Benjamin Watson, Pamela D. Drayton
and Philip Rail of PEOPLE tearsheets; Time-Life Photo Lab;
Yaron Fidler Production Studio; Dennis Ortiz-Lopez.

✷ ✷ ✷

A Fawcett Columbine Book
Published by Ballantine Books

This edition published simultaneously in hardcover by
Time-Life Books Inc., Alexandria, Virginia

Library of Congress Catalog Card Number: 83-91118
ISBN 0-449-90113-0

Cover and book design: Gregory B. Leeds

Manufactured in the United States of America

First Ballantine Books Edition: March 1984
10 9 8 7 6 5 4 3 2 1

CONTENTS

INTRODUCTION

HARRY BENSON

The magazine's publisher and managing editors present and past: from left, Dick Durrell, Pat Ryan, Dick Stolley.

Richard B. Stolley, whose comments appear below, was the managing editor of PEOPLE *from its first issue until March 1982, when he became the managing editor of* LIFE.

The most significant development in American publishing in the past decade has been the evolution of "personality journalism"—reporting and photography that concentrate on individuals. PEOPLE magazine, which was launched in March 1974, is generally credited with bringing the term into the language and personality journalism into full flower.

Now everybody's doing it. Newspapers devote entire sections to people in the news. The gossip column has made a dramatic comeback. Television has spawned *Real People* and *Entertainment Tonight*. More and more magazines are running celebrities on their covers, even the women's service magazines. Whatever happened to chocolate cake and needlepoint?

Well, one explanation is that needlepoint isn't nearly as much fun as human beings. We all know that people say, think and do the darndest things. For a decade now, PEOPLE has been there to capture all this in words and pictures. From this weekly celebration of humanity comes *The Best of People, The First Decade.* A reader who can get through these pages without a smile (even a belly laugh) of recognition or pleasure or nostalgia is made of stern stuff.

Although PEOPLE's kind of journalism seems new, it actually began a long time ago, and is as much a part of mainstream American journalism as investigative reporting or editorial comment. Writing about personalities predates journalism itself by a couple of millennia. Henry Luce once observed of the magazine he founded in 1923: "TIME didn't invent stories about people; the Bible did."

But we have to ask: Do we need personality journalism now and in the future? I think we do. The reporting of intimate facts, which is at the heart of personality journalism, contributes without question to our understanding and judgment of popular leaders in politics, the arts, entertainment, business. Journalists often cite Chappaquiddick in 1969 as the benchmark, the event that made them realize how much they knew about what was really going on in the lives of prominent people, but which they rarely reported. Then there was Watergate. If vindication of personality journalism was ever needed, Watergate provided it. Without responsible keyhole reporting on the Watergate figures, we might never have comprehended the enormity of their misbehavior or the absence of their remorse.

But how much personality journalism is enough? How much is too much? Will the day arrive when the country will OD on celebrities, when we may need a warning from the Surgeon General that news of, say, Farrah Fawcett is dangerous to your health?

I see no evidence that this kind of situation is at hand. On the contrary, PEOPLE has increasingly tackled the important political, economic and social issues in the world through the men and women caught up in them.

The responsibility that comes with our freedom to practice personality journalism, or any other kind, has been an issue in this country since its founding. Thomas Jefferson's anguish over the question led him to propose, with all seriousness, that an editor divide his publication into four sections: truths, probabilities, possibilities and lies. PEOPLE has an obvious responsibility to the truth—in our case, that fragile merchandise, the facts about another human being.

We have an obligation to readers too. The desire for publicity can be insatiable, which means we have to avoid being manipulated. The proliferation of personality journalism has spawned a disturbing trend as some celebrities have sought to control stories done on them. In return for giving a publication time, letting themselves be photographed and answering sometimes imperti-

nent questions, these prominent men and women demand to be consulted about the pictures and text. Readers have a stake in this matter of journalistic ethics: When a publication gives in to these demands, its credibility is lost and readers lose too.

Oriana Fallaci, the Italian interviewer, is fond of saying that journalists are historians. Her comment raises a question for all of us: To what extent *is* journalism history? To what extent should we be historically conscious of what we are doing? Historians can point to Boswell and Herodotus, whose classic literature centered on intimate details of the people they were writing about: whom they saw, what they said, whom they loved, etc.

I think PEOPLE can legitimately claim to be putting out a record of our times that is both historical and unique. For the past decade our editorial job has been to describe the way we are. How we speak and about what. What we wear. Our attitudes toward one another, toward our leaders, toward children. The fads, the heroes, the goats. In other words, popular culture in its broadest sense. Each week PEOPLE gives a portrait of the world through the human beings that inhabit it. In our first decade, we reported on some 20,000 citizens of all ages, races, nationalities, temperaments and prominence. At least half of them were ordinary people doing extraordinary things. Perhaps, when all is said and done, they are the Best of People. In our first issue, dated March 4, 1974, our introductory editors' note said:

"We want to reflect the times. . . . Editorially, we hope to come at everything fresh. To reassess the old familiar faces. To welcome the new and eager. To peer into the lives of the hitherto undiscovered. And to do all this with zest, sensitivity and good humor. Believe us," we concluded, "quote us, enjoy us." Those of you who have bought more than 1.12 billion copies of PEOPLE seem to have done so.

Mia Farrow was the editors' choice for the first cover, dated March 4, 1974. The issue sold a total of 976,000 copies.

MARY ANNE FACKELMAN/THE WHITE HOUSE

LEADERS

MAKING A PASS

President Reagan gave a campaign smooch to Nancy during his 1976 run for office, and later, in 1982, he good-humoredly struck a Gipper-like stance in the White House.

They are Presidents and Prime Ministers, men of faith and violent fanatics, monarchs as well as common people caught up in uncommon roles. They are the leaders, the movers and shakers whose deeds have helped shape the world during PEOPLE's first decade. And, whether viewed in the calm of the White House rose garden or in the hot spots of the Middle East, all were the focus of intensive, close-up reporting that sought to look beyond public posturing to the real men and women beneath.

IN THE SWIM

Photographer Dick Swanson took the plunge in 1975 in order to get a *Jaws*-eye view of President Ford in the new White House swimming pool.

LEADERS

IN THE TANK

Jimmy Carter's near collapse during a 1979 road race threw a scare into White House doctor William Lukash (right) and accompanying Secret Service agents.

LEADERS

ENGLAND'S IRON LADY

Her tough Tory policies earned Margaret Thatcher the nickname "Attila the Hen," but her lighter side was revealed at a 1979 boat show. In 1983 she easily won reelection.

BEATING A RAP

Convicted of breaking election laws in 1975, India's Prime Minister Indira Gandhi, daughter of Jawaharlal Nehru, responded by cracking down on opponents and the press.

UNDER DURESS

Shortly before the Polish
government outlawed his
union, devout shipyard
worker-turned-Solidarity
leader Lech Walesa
confessed to a priest
in Warsaw.

POLISH PAPA

Scholar and poet, John
Paul II in 1978 became the
first Polish priest called to
be Pope. From Rome he
leads the world's 720 million Roman Catholics.

LEADERS

ISLAMIC EXTREMIST

"I was chosen by God to perform a task," said Iran's Ayatollah Khomeini, whose labors in 1979 included taking 53 Americans hostage.

ISRAEL'S HARD-LINER

Polish-born Menachem Begin dominated Israeli politics as Prime Minister from 1977 to 1983 when, at 70, he announced, "I cannot carry on," and retired.

PALESTINIAN POINT MAN

PLO Chairman Yasser Arafat talked tough at a 1974 Arab summit but by 1983 he had to abandon Beirut and faced revolt from Syria-backed rebels.

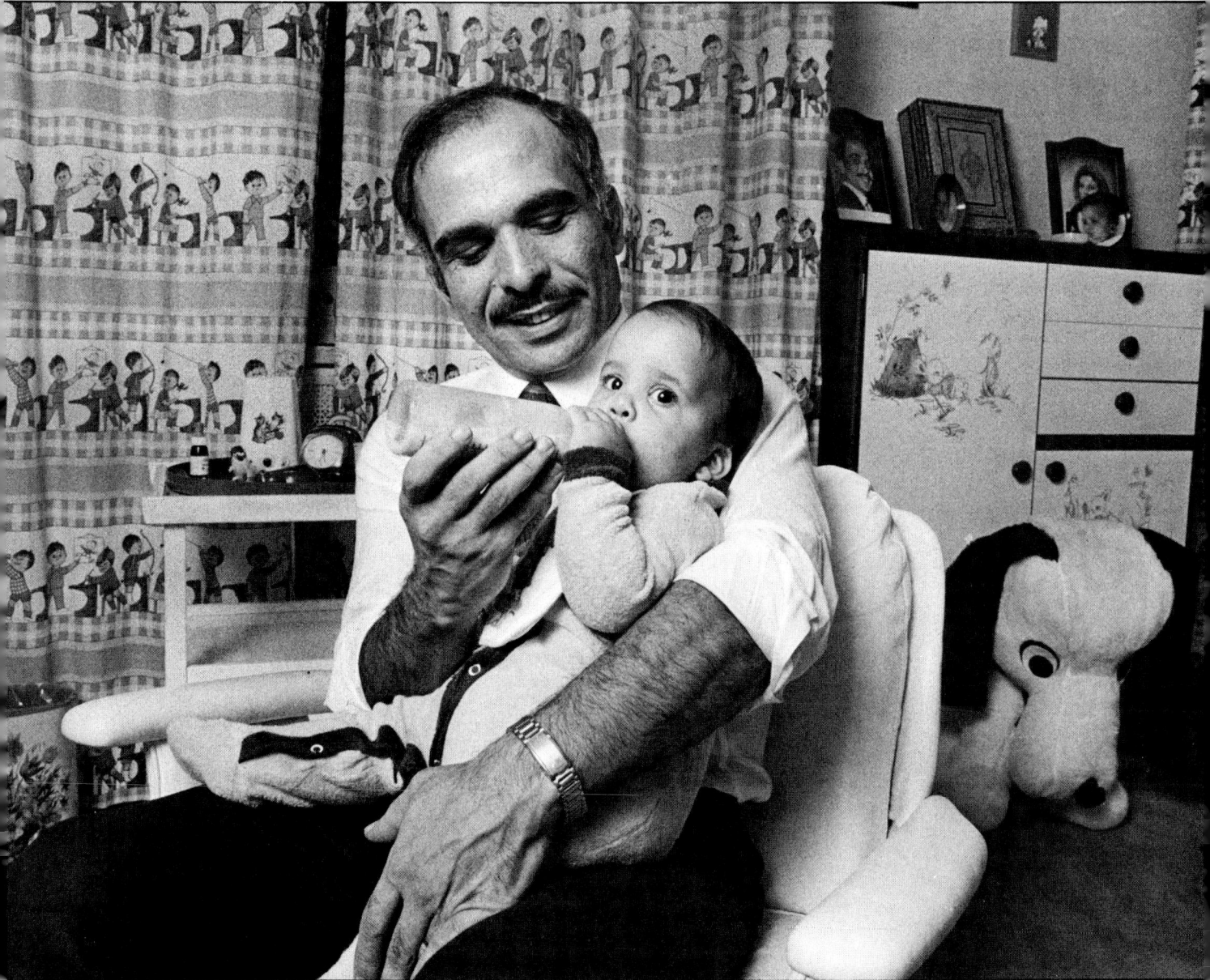

PLUCKY LITTLE KING

Jordan's King Hussein gave baby Princess Haya some royal treatment in 1975. Made a widower soon after, he married American Lisa Halaby and increased his brood to 10.

TIME TO GO

At the end of his goodbyes to the staff on his last day as President in 1974, Richard Nixon stood beside Pat, head down, crying softly. Suddenly he weaved, stumbled, and aides had to steady him. Then he left the room.

HARRY BENSON

THE BEST OF TIMES THE WORST OF TIMES

As Charles Dickens wrote in *A Tale of Two Cities* of another time more than a century ago, it was also "the age of wisdom, it was the age of foolishness, it was the epoch of belief, it was the epoch of incredulity…it was the spring of hope, it was the winter of despair."

In our decade, one President quit, another filled in, a third strode on in triumph and off in disaster, leaving the fourth to try managing the nation.

Words, too, came and went. "10" became a new sort of knockout, "roots" and "boogie" came back big, and a motley band of strangers barged in: toxic waste, Symbionese Liberation Army, Studio 54, Moral Majority, Agent Orange, Bicentennial, Moonies, minimarathons, Three Mile Island.

And belatedly, with quarrels, a memorial was dedicated in Washington to the dead of a non-war, which for many Vietnam vets sadly still had not come to an end.

BEST OF TIMES
WORST OF TIMES

GRAND OLD PARTY

Hours after being acquitted of conspiracy in 1974, ex-Attorney General John Mitchell celebrated with his lawyers. In 1977 he was jailed for perjury and fraud over Watergate (serving 19 months) and the parties ended.

LOVE'S OLD SWEET SONG

Separated from John, bubbly Martha Mitchell, who made her flamboyance famous, flashed the old form for a photographer in 1974. She died of cancer two years later.

STEVEN WEED/SYGMA

20

MARK GODFREY/ARCHIVE

COMING OF AGE AS A COMMUNIST

Angela Davis, Girl Scout turned Communist and college teacher, railed at prison racism in 1974: "How wrong!" Tried for the 1970 murder of a judge and three others, then cleared, she won a 1978 Lenin Peace Prize.

GROWING UP IN AMERICA

Patty Hearst looked demure before she was grabbed by the SLA in '74, became "Tanya," was jailed for nearly two years, called her kidnappers "just rats," wed her policeman bodyguard, Bernard Shaw, and began a family.

21

BEST OF TIMES
WORST OF TIMES

SHUTTLE DIPLOMACY

A global power by himself, Henry Kissinger ran State, negotiated Vietnam and the Mideast, and in 1975, at 52, found peace with wife Nancy, who helicoptered with him and popped his pomp with jokes.

APOCALYPSE NOW

Exiled from Russia in '74, Nobel-winner Aleksandr Solzhenitsyn was still steeped in doom a decade later ("the entire 20th century is sucked into self-destruction") and denounced repression on all fronts.

23

BEST OF TIMES
WORST OF TIMES

MICHAEL MAUNEY

SELF-
"TO BE∧ EVIDENT"

Helping celebrate the Bicentennial, John Chancellor recreated Thomas Jefferson's struggles to word the Declaration of Independence just right.

ROOTS BOOSTER

In print and on TV, *Roots* made ethnic heritage the rage and Alex Haley rich and sought after, especially by women but, he sighed in Gambia, he'd sooner "be famous one day a month."

ARTHUR SCHATZ

ALAIN NOGUES-SYGMA

AFRICAN HARVEST

"I am very, very discouraged," said Dr. Norman Borlaug, "Father of the Green Revolution," in 1974 as agronomy failed to check famine, and bran, airlifted in to feed cattle, was scavenged for food by sub-Sahara families.

BEST OF TIMES
WORST OF TIMES

HARRY BENSON

NEW SMOOTHIE

After her husband, Jerry, left the White House, Betty Ford cured her alcohol problem, got a lift and became, as Bob Hope said, "the only new face in the Republican Party."

JAILHOUSE ROCK

Steve Rubell (left) had time for Halston and Margaux Hemingway at his Studio 54 in 1977, but no time for lowly boogie-ers ("You're ugly, I don't want you here"), and later did time for dodging taxes.

SHAKING FREE

Sick of "being public property," mercurial Maggie Trudeau by 1978 had ditched (but not divorced) "my truest one," Canadian PM Pierre, in favor of acting, discoing and other wiggles.

ROBIN PLATZER, IMAGES

28

BEST OF TIMES
WORST OF TIMES

HARRY BENSON

GREG ROBINSON/SAN FRANCISCO EXAMINER

DEATH IN THE AFTERNOON

"A madman with charisma," an ex-follower called cult leader Jim Jones. "I curse the day I was born," Jones himself said. On Nov. 18, 1978 he led 912 of his disciples in Guyana to suicide by Grape Flavor Aid and cyanide.

PROPOSITION MAKER

A salty-tongued Mormon who began his days with a belt of vodka, Howard Jarvis, 75, had his giddiest day in 1978: After trying 16 years, he saw California okay his Proposition 13 to slash property taxes.

©1983 JULIAN WASSER

AIR OF DANGER

A year after the threat of
nuclear disaster at Three
Mile Island terrified the
nation in 1979, chemical
waste specialist Michael
Brown visited Elizabeth,
N.J., where a warehouse of
toxic leftovers had erupt-
ed in a 200-foot fireball.

BEN WEAVER/CAMERA 5

FOAM, SWEET FOAM

Small peanuts to some and a royal pain to others, kid brother Billy Carter guzzled and guffawed his way to better'n $500,000 in 1977, using the back of his gas station as HQ.

JAY: LEVITON-ATLANTA

34

BILL FITZ-PATRICK/THE WHITE HOUSE

PRIVATE SESSION

Rosalynn Carter (with grandchild Sarah) loved "the intrigues of politics" but kept pressure away from the White House second floor. "Up there," she said, "we're a family."

PEACE WORK

Camp David brought Menachem Begin and Anwar Sadat together with their driven, patient mediator, President Jimmy Carter, for one shining moment.

SWIFT JUSTICE IN IRAN

After a 90-minute trial in 1979 by a holy man known as "Judge Blood," 11 Kurdish rebels and agents of Iran's ousted Shah fell before the firing squad of another holy man, the Ayatollah Khomeini.

BEST OF TIMES
WORST OF TIMES

DICK SWANSON

COMEBACK TRAIL

A bullet John Hinckley meant for President Reagan cost Jim Brady part of his frontal brain tissue but, a year later, still in daily therapy, the gritty, gallant press secretary enjoyed kidding with his son Scott.

DEATH PASSES BY

Wincing as he was hit, Ronald Reagan in April, 1981, became the fifth President to be shot but his wit was unharmed. "Please tell me that you're Republicans," he joked in the operating room.

BRUCE McBROOM

PEEK-A-BO

Her liquid undulations
made Bo Derek the No. 1
sex goddess in *10*. Then
John Derek's 1979 best-
selling poster shot of her,
still dripping, made him
the No. 1 wife-snapper.

CO RENTMEESTER

REVVING UP
THE RIGHT

**The Rev. Jerry Falwell led
his Moral Majority vs. wel-
fare, abortion, ERA and, in
1980, Bayh (Ind.), McGov-
ern (S.Dak) and Church
(Id.). The liberals all lost.**

41

HONORABLY DISCHARGED

In 1974, six years and some 40 operations after he was horribly wounded in Vietnam, his face partially destroyed, hardly able to talk or eat, ex-Pfc. Rory Bailey waited in an Illinois R.R. station, his face covered to spare strangers he could not see. Before going to Vietnam, he had been just another smiling draftee; since 1974, more surgery has enabled him to eat solid foods and move slowly toward the quiet life he seeks.

MICHAEL MAUNEY

Fads & Follies

A deliciously weird, wacky, wonderful decade! It came in with streaking, gathered speed with jogging and skateboarding, and ended up ballooning. People walked Pet Rocks and checked out emotions with Mood Stones. There were demonstrations of the human spirit (George Willig scaled the World Trade Center), of persistence (Bob Speca proved out the domino theory—97,500 times), and patience (until Ernö Rubik unleashed his Cube). Ingenuity extended even to do-it-yourself coffins, which, as a Valley Girl would say, is grody to the max.

STREAKING

In 1974, British bobbies gave hats-offs aid to Michael O'Brien, an accountant, while 50,000 rugby fans roared their approval.

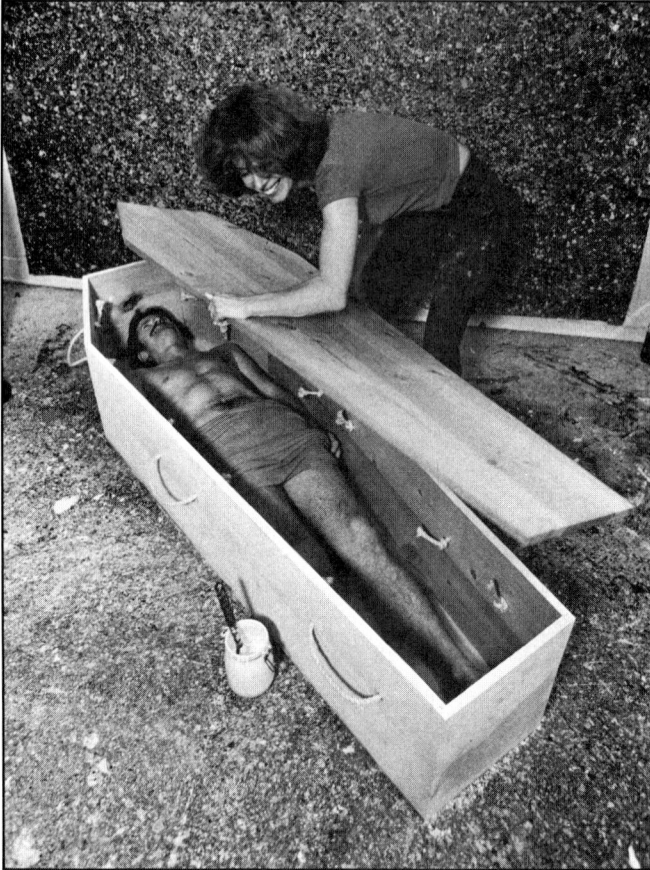

CB RADIOS

Former Omaha adman Bill Fries (atop cab) rode his 1976 hit, *Convoy,* to the top of the charts and helped all good buddies to keep the electronic boom rolling.

DO-IT-YOURSELF COFFINS

Plain pine boxes were good for napping in 1978, but the real reason two Episcopal priests sold them was to put a lid on the high cost of dying.

RUBIK'S CUBE

America became a nation of cubic rubes in 1981 thanks to Hungarian Ernö Rubik, the architecture professor whose puzzle boasted 43 quintillion possible combinations.

MOOD STONE RINGS

One-time stockbroker Josh Reynolds bolstered his assets in 1975 by creating a temperature-sensitive bijou that, he claimed, could reveal the wearer's mood and state of mind.

Fads & Follies

PAC-MAN

Its name came from the Japanese "paku," meaning "to eat," and in 1982 Pac-Man gobbled up Scott Baio (above) and a lion's share of the $6-billion business in video games.

PET ROCKS

"You might say we've packaged a sense of humor," said Gary Dahl whose $4 egg-shaped Mexican beach stones sold at the peak rate of 100,000 per day in 1975.

Fads & Follies

JOHN G. ZIMMERMAN

SKATEBOARDING

In 1978, Tony "Mad Dog" Alva, 20, was lord of the little board that gave "hamburgers" (lumps) to 335,000 not-so-good skates.

ROLLER SKATING

Cher (with disco whiz Bill Butler) had the figure for eights in '79, when the polyurethane wheel had 28 million Americans spinning.

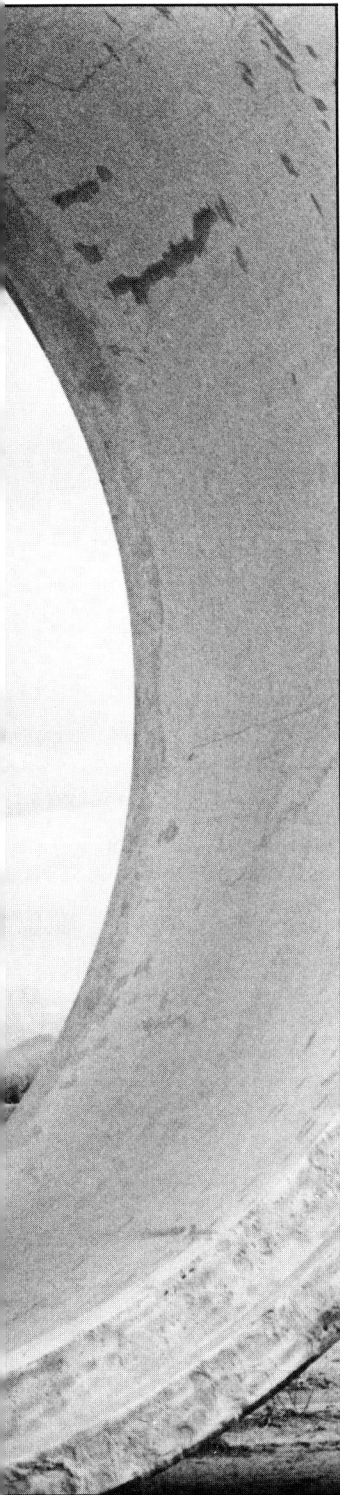

TEENY BIKE

What's 3.9 inches long, fits in a glove compartment, runs for 15 minutes and was created by Raino Frischknecht, the man who also gave the world the motorized violin case? This.

49

Fads & Follies

DALE WITTNER

FAT CAT DELUXE

"He's a little bit of Archie Bunker and Morris the Cat tossed together," said creator Jim Davis of Garfield, the tubby tabby who clawed his way onto America's best-seller lists.

STEVE NORTHUP

BANG!

DRAWING FIRE

Cartoonist Simon Bond took a volley from fans of felines for his book, *101 Uses for a Dead Cat*. Among his far-out notions: using kitties littered about as rugs.

PAUL DeGRUCCIO/SHOOTING STAR

MOUSEKET-EARS

Residents of Sun City, Ariz. were all ears, thanks to Edgar Sims (second from right). His mousy ears for the hard-of-hearing were "based on the principle of people cupping their hands around the ear."

50

BRUCE W. TALAMON

DARIO PERLA

THOMAS S. ENGLAND

IN THE CHIPS

After 13 years as a talent agent, Wally Amos finally found a recipe for success from his Aunt Della. The result? A nationwide craving for the Famous Amos Chocolate Chip Cookie.

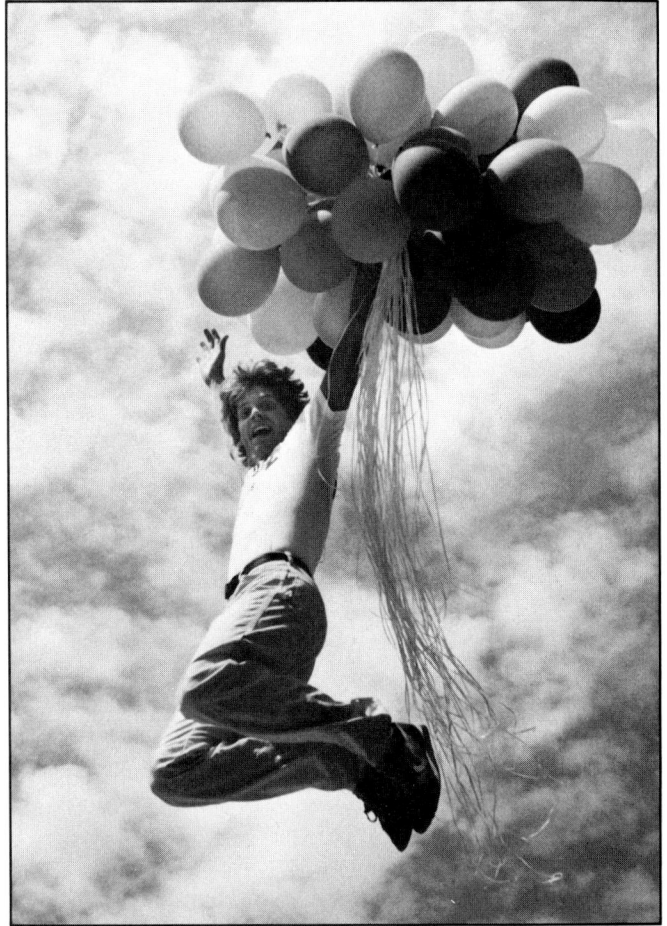

HIGH HO!

For those tired of sending the usual ho-hum bunch of flowers, L.A.'s Steve Blunck in 1980 offered something different: a bouquet of balloons.

PURE CORN

"I provide the hot air," joked Orville Redenbacher of the 1978 TV ads that turned his pricey Gourmet Popping Corn into a $30-million-a-year business.

Fads & Follies

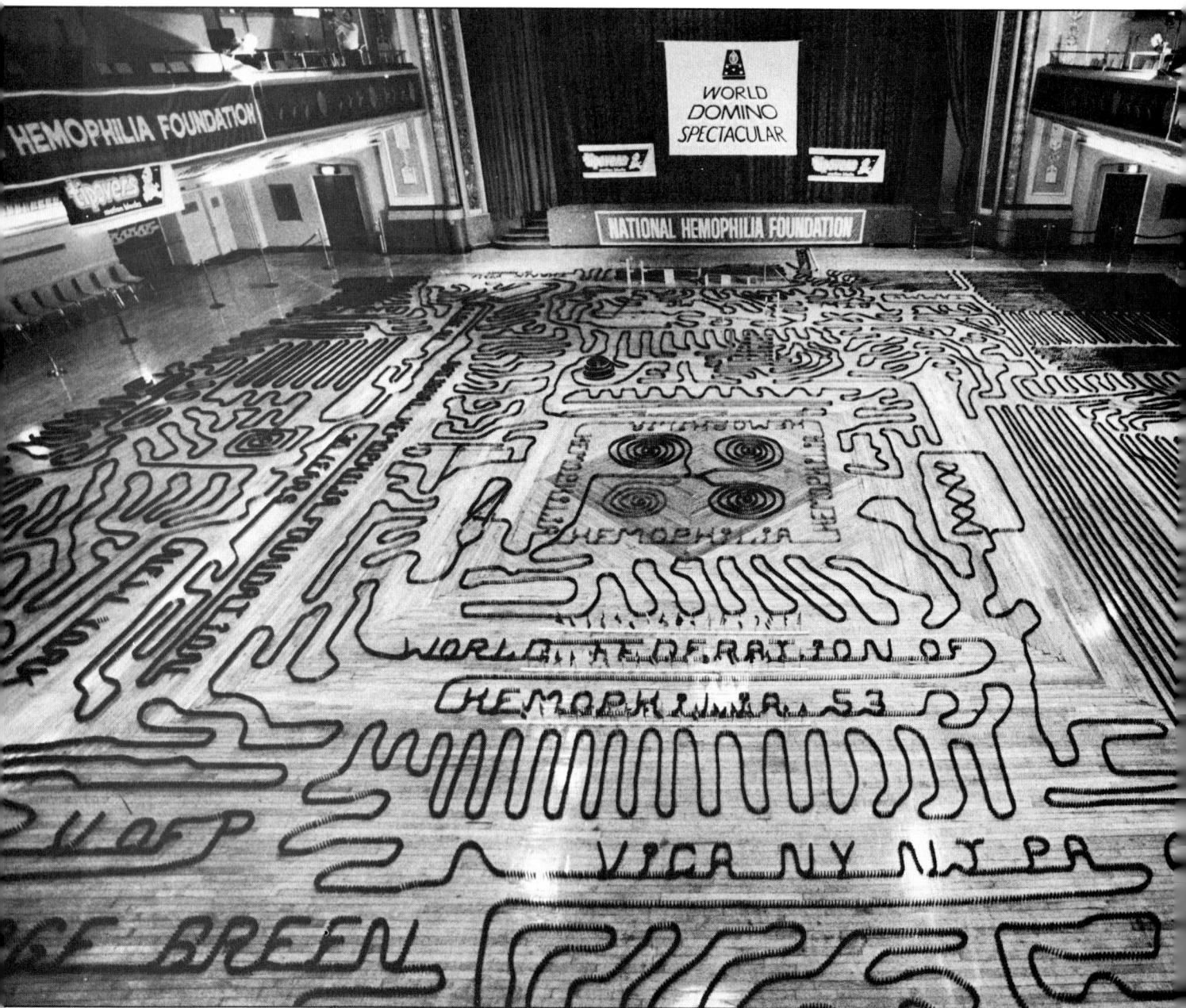

HENRY GROSKINSKY

AND UH-ONE AND UH-TWO ...

There were 100,000—count 'em—dominoes standing when Bob Speca Jr. started, and 97,500 toppled before he set the world record in 1978. A klutzy ABC-TV cameraman felled the rest.

HEMOPHILIA FOUNDATION

KONG, SCHMONG

Modest George Willig climbed up the World Trade Center in 1977 and said, shrugging, "People just get excited when a common guy does something uncommon."

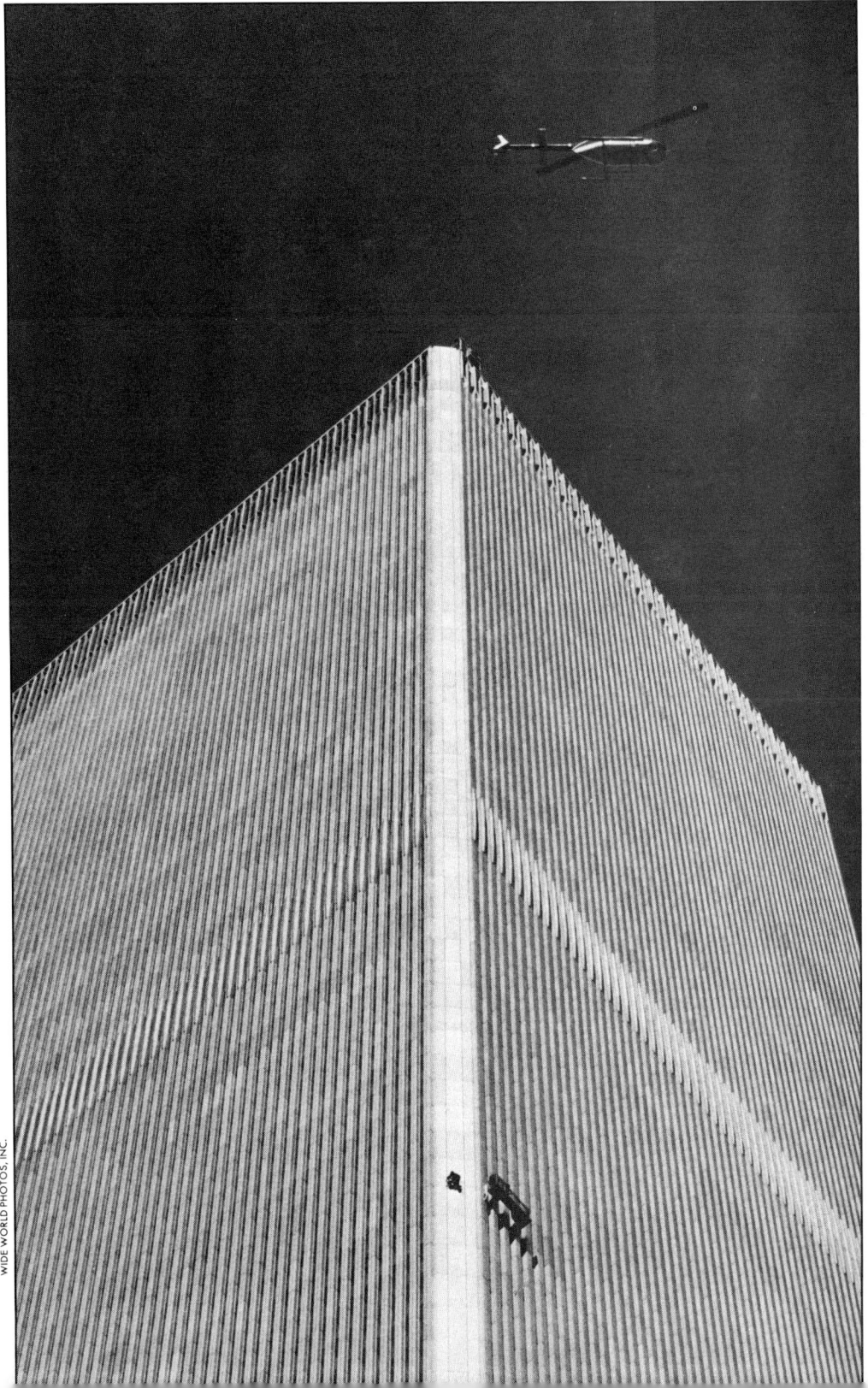

Fads & Follies

FOWL PLAY

Arizonan Ed McWilliams thought he was on target with his outsized decoys, but a local federal warden ruled for the birds and shot down the idea.

THINKING BIG

New York artist Kevin O'Callaghan tried a 13-foot sample case to get his stalled career rolling.

DOWNBEAT

High school drummer Patrick Fioravanti used his head in a 1982 band competition in Oklahoma.

PRESS ASSOCIATION LTD.

CLOUDHOPPER

**Englishman Colin Prescot
in 1980 hoped a $6,000
hot-air balloon (complete
with emergency para-
chute) would get off the
ground with London's grid-
locked commuters.**

COUPLES

Through eternal vows and agonizing splits, long-run loves and brief encounters, alimony, palimony, scandal and all sorts of advice, marriage American-style showed that there are still ties that bind.

BUTTEFUL WHILE IT LASTED

Actress-singer Ronee Blakley and German film director Wim Wenders wed idyllically on Lizard Butte near her hometown of Caldwell, Idaho in 1979. Now the bad news: they split after 12 months.

EARL BROCKMAN

Couples

I THEE MERGE

Bill Agee, boss of Bendix, denied romance with Mary Cunningham, his VP. She quit, became a Seagram VP, wed Agee in 1981 and said, "I'm 31 and, God, what I've been through."

A MARITAL ART

In 28 years as the pundit's wife, literary agent Ann Buchwald learned how to stifle Art, to the envy of every pol he's ever skewered. "He's about as malleable as our front porch," she declared.

LOVE AMONG THE ASHES

"It is not easy for a well-known person to choose the right words," said Arthur Ashe, goofing his first meeting with photog Jeanne Moutoussamy. With Andrew Young presiding, "I do" later worked.

COUPLES

An Olympic hero's ex-wife finally drops her torch

They were to all appearances the golden couple of American sport: Bruce Jenner, the boyishly handsome Olympic hero, and his stunning blond wife, Chrystie, who worked as a stewardess to support Bruce while he trained for the 1976 decathlon. But after the birth of their first child in 1978, their marriage began to fall apart. Bruce became increasingly restless; Chrystie felt frustrated since she had stopped working to raise their son. Counseling and an attempt at reconciliation having failed, Chrystie talked to Stephen Smuin for PEOPLE about the agony of divorce.

Had it not been for the demands of our new wealth and our concern over what people were thinking, our marriage might have had a better chance. But I am not totally convinced we'd still be together because we're such different people. Bruce was the first to admit it. He'd say, "I am treating you terribly and I don't know why." Now he has achieved a certain public status and has a power with other people that is very alluring. You don't get money and fame without paying for it, with time or with your soul.

We tried our hardest to patch it together. I was very impressed with how open and honest Bruce was during therapy—much more than he had ever been. But there is no patching it together if someone is in love with somebody else. I needed to know if he was in love with Linda Thompson. He said yes, and he wanted a divorce. No ifs, ands or buts about it. I just fell apart. I kept asking, "How could he give me up that easily?"

Many women have had trouble with my being so devoted to Bruce's winning the gold medal. Yes, I had to subjugate everything, but it was a goal I wanted as badly as Bruce. Now I see it's everybody's responsibility to set limits about what will be sacrificed in a marriage. To live through some-body else was extremely frustrating.

The power of money is so damned destructive. When people are making as much money as Bruce, they just think they can do what they want. I was making the money for a long time in our relationship, but I didn't use it as a source of power against him. After our son, Burt, was born I used to tell Bruce how powerless and undignified I felt having no earning power. I hated that feeling. Prior to the Olympics it was "our money"; afterwards it became "his" money.

I really feel many of these problems would have come about in any marriage. It wasn't just that Bruce was a famous athlete. It was the fact of my growing as a woman. You sell a package when you get married: I can cook, I can entertain, I can look good, I can be good in bed, I can do all these things. In a way I deceived Bruce about who I was. I didn't know who I was so I sold him what I thought he wanted. My own insecurity said, "If he finds out who I am, will he want me?" If I'd voiced my needs more, our marriage might have had a greater chance.

After living through the divorce negotiations, I would advise other women to make their own decisions. A divorce is often the first time women ever take any control—most don't know about insurance policies or stocks or whatever. I didn't feel this way when the divorce began. I was very concerned that Bruce think well of me. I thought that if I stepped quietly out the back door he would always say what a nice girl I was. Then I began to realize that regardless of what I took or did not take, he wasn't going to speak highly of me.

This has changed my relationship with men. I don't give anything now, but I receive a lot. I look for somebody that puts no demands on me at all. The pressure of making somebody else happy is too much. That is one of the reasons I would hesitate to remarry. My fulfillment 10 years ago was totally through a man. Today the important things in my life are my kids, my interior design work, my friends and my running, and I feel fulfilled by those. My future is very bright. I'm not this sad, helpless, weak martyr that has been depicted in the press. I know I will succeed: It's just a matter of time.
January 12, 1981

Subsequently, Bruce married Elvis Presley's former girlfriend, Linda Thompson. Chrystie started an interior decorating business and married attorney Richard Scott.

"I had grown familiar with the role of victim," said Chrystie, with son Burt, 2, and daughter Cassandra, whom husband Bruce had once tried to persuade her to abort.

©1981 TONY KORODY/SYGMA

WILLIAM HOLDEN AND STEFANIE POWERS

Touching scenes from a Hollywood love story

In 1977 Bill and Stef happily made do in his still unfinished Palm Springs aerie. "I only had him for nine years," she later mourned after his tragic death in 1981.

I was thrilled," William Holden was saying, sounding not at all like a man who had just lost the 1977 Academy Award. "The greatest memorial anyone can have is the way he's remembered, and the Oscar will be part of our memory of Peter Finch. I can't tell you how happy I was it happened that way." The reaction to the posthumous award to his *Network* co-star was characteristically civil and generous: Holden has a reputation for being both. In a film career spanning nearly four decades, Hollywood has spilled its every treasure at his feet: scores of leading roles, an Oscar for *Stalag 17* in 1954, fame beyond mere celebrity.

If Hollywood has any promise left to keep, it is that his 34-year-old lover, Stefanie Powers, achieve some measure of the acting success that he, at 58, has come to take in stride. "Stef is young and underrated," he says. "Her break can be ahead of her." But she remains skeptical. "My heart is blacker than Bill's," she says. "I don't think it's going to happen."

Although both are products of Hollywood, they are anything but its prototype couple. They see each other mainly on weekends, when he drives to her house in L.A.'s Benedict Canyon or she to his in Palm Springs. "Marriage isn't a consideration at all," Holden says. "Why ruin it?" Powers agrees. "Our visits are properly spaced so that each of us can go off on our own tangents." Those tangents, they say, are not amorous; notwithstanding the 24-year age difference and their disinterest in marriage, their relationship is based on fidelity. (Holden enjoys being gallantly oblique about how they make it work. "We have a very well-balanced relationship," he says. "You can read into that whatever you like.")

The relationship seems to flourish with the distance they put between themselves and Hollywood during frequent trips to Kenya, where he owns an interest in a 1,256-acre game ranch, and New Guinea, where she buys native works for import and sale. Their first such jaunt, after discovering each other over the anthropology bin in an L.A. bookshop in 1974, was to Hong Kong,

where Holden had investments. Within a year they had traveled to Malaya, Singapore, Iran, Europe, New Guinea and then Africa for a weeks-long "game capture." Two dozen animals—elephants, rhinos, elands and zebras—were caught, vaccinated and hauled off to Holden's preserve on the slopes of snow-capped Mount Kenya. Recalls Don Hunt, who runs the game ranch: "In time Stefanie became adept at wrestling a wildly kicking zebra to the ground, and Bill in a speeding truck was more skillful with a two-inch-thick rope lasso than in any of his cowboy roles."

Powers, born Stefania Zofia Federkiewicz, wanted to be an archeologist but her mother encouraged her to audition for movies—as many of her Hollywood High classmates were doing. She eventually did 15 films, running to such juvenilia as *The Interns* and *Palm Springs Weekend.* In 1966 she married actor Gary Lockwood and they were amicably divorced in 1974.

By the time Holden met Stefanie that year, he had been divorced from former actress Brenda Marshall for 11 years. (They have two grown sons.) From his first role in *Golden Boy* in 1939 through his best work in *Sunset Boulevard, Country Girl* and *Sabrina* in the '50s, Holden both profited and suffered from a marvelously impulsive spirit. (It had led him, as an upper-crust teenager in Pasadena, to walk the outside railing of a bridge on his hands on a dare.) When direc-

tor Joshua Logan balked at letting him do his own stunts in *Picnic* in 1956, Holden hung from an eighth-floor ledge until Logan relented. He could also empathize with Powers' despair in the shallows of her profession. "In the early 1960s," he recalls, "I didn't work for three years." And although he made $2.5 million on *Bridge on the River Kwai* (he takes it in $50,000 annual installments), he can understand working for hard cash alone. "I'm still not in a position to do just what I want to do," he admits. Certainly it isn't the social life that keeps them in Hollywood. "We're not party people," says Holden. "We're involved with the doers, the accomplishers. If our friends aren't scholars, they're goddamn good students."

Their big dream is a car trip through the Yucatan peninsula. "Like that line in *Network,* 'I'm a lot closer to the end than I am to the beginning, so I don't intend to waste any time,'" Holden has said. "We always have trips planned, Stef and I. There's so much to see, after all, so bloody much to learn."

April 11, 1977

Two years after the above story ran, Powers won the fame Holden wished for her on TV's Hart to Hart. In November 1981, Bill Holden died at 63 of head injuries sustained in a fall in his apartment. Six months later Stefanie took over the environmental work in Kenya that he loved. "The ranch is Bill's memorial," she said.

COUPLES

Their marriage survived her affair and a shocking lawsuit

Our marriage started out just like anyone else's. —Larry King

For Larry and Billie Jean King, who in the fall of 1981 would celebrate their 16th wedding anniversary, events that spring were a cruel undoing. For much of their married lives, they had devoted themselves to the cause of women's tennis. He was the organization man and entrepreneur; she was the symbol, the star, the foremost female athlete of her time. Her achievements had gone far beyond her record 20 Wimbledon trophies and her 12 Grand Slam singles titles and all the other prizes her sport had heaped on her. With Larry's business savvy, she converted the game of women's tennis from a nickel-and-dime sideshow into a $10-million circuit, organized a players' union (the Women's Tennis Association), started a magazine *(womenSports)* and underwrote a women's professional softball team. The parity with men's tennis and the lucrative endorsement contracts women players enjoy could not have happened except for the trailblazing Kings.

And then the unthinkable happened: the sudden emergence of an embarrassing bit of wreckage from their all but discarded private lives. It was served up to the press in the form of a titillating lawsuit from Marilyn Barnett, 33, Billie Jean's former hairdresser and secretary, who claimed to have had a seven-year lesbian relationship with her boss that entitled her to the Kings' Malibu home and half of Billie Jean's earnings during their years together, estimated at more than $1 million. Brandishing scores of love letters in support of her charges, Barnett thus brought the clamor of spectacle to a subject on which silence had long been the most pragmatic policy. In doing so, she left both Larry and Billie Jean King feeling the indignity of public exposure, the pain of a former intimate's betrayal—and the fear that their achievements and hopes for the future had been gravely jeopardized.

At the bottom of it was a woman scorned. A graduate of Beverly Hills High, the only daughter of a studio publicist, Marilyn Barnett first met Billie Jean in 1972, when she was recommended by a friend to cut King's hair. Soon Barnett accepted a job as her personal assistant and ad hoc road manager. She kept Billie Jean's schedule, bought her clothes, chauffeured her to appointments—and, after the two women became lovers, shared her hotel rooms, often with Larry staying just down the hall. In 1974 Marilyn went back to work as a hairdresser with the Jon Peters Beauty Salon in Beverly Hills and convinced the Kings to buy the $135,000 beach house in Malibu. There Marilyn set up housekeeping and continued to enjoy a luxurious life, in part with the Kings' credit cards.

She was far from a trouble-free houseguest. In the previous two years she had been rushed to the hospital at least three times for apparent drug abuse. In October 1980, she had jumped 25 feet off the deck of the house in Malibu onto the beach in an unsuccessful suicide attempt. The others had left her uninjured. This one fractured her spine. "The doctors have told me that they don't know if I will ever be able to walk again," said Marilyn, who had applied for Social Security benefits.

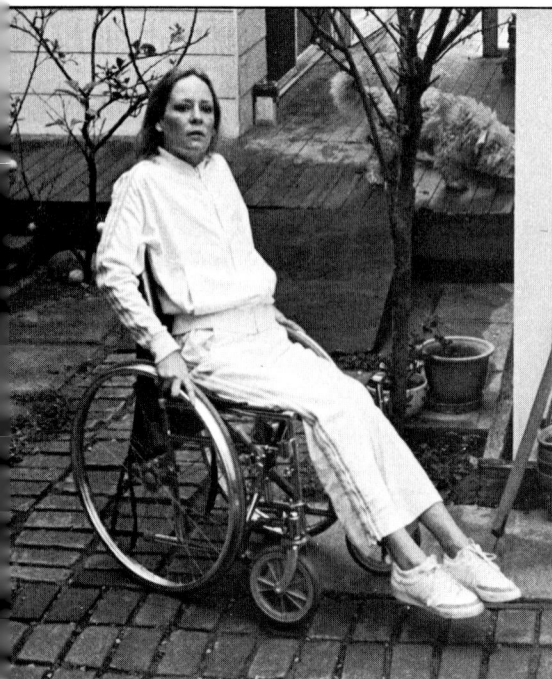

Disabled by a spinal injury, Marilyn Barnett used a wheelchair, but she was able to walk into the courtroom for the trial.

To escape the publicity about her liaison with

Astonishingly, Larry King admitted that he had known of his wife's relationship with Barnett all along—and accepted it, submerging his jealousy in his and Billie Jean's overriding ambitions for the sport and for the empire they were building together. As their shock wore off, the Kings sat down with PEOPLE senior writer Cheryl McCall, a longtime friend and former managing editor of *womenSports,* and reflected with moving candor on how Barnett's revelations had affected them and their marriage. Billie Jean (BJK) opened the interview:

BJK: The day the news of Marilyn's suit broke I went into shock. I just screamed. Larry was the only one for admitting it right away. I was worried about my parents, but I still have to live with myself first.

LK: Billie Jean's first reaction was to pack. When I got there, all the bags were packed. I wondered what was going on.

BJK: I told Larry, "I've got to get the hell out of here. This is it. This is going to ruin so many things I've worked for, so many dreams I've had for tennis."

LK: I knew Marilyn was threatening two days before that. Our lawyer called and said the agreement Marilyn and her lawyer want is the house and financial support for the rest of her life. Basically they said, "Pay this money or we'll sue you."

Marilyn Barnett, Billie Jean and Larry sought safe haven in their Marina del Rey apartment.

BJK: I said, "You've got to be kidding! That's blackmail." I told Larry I wasn't going to live the rest of my life being blackmailed. It's just not worth it. When I publicly admitted the affair with Marilyn, I expected the absolute worst and decided anything less than that would be fortunate.

LK: Everyone's biggest concern is that somehow Billie Jean will be proselytizing other players to be gay, and that's not the way she is at all. It's not contagious. I didn't catch it.

BJK: I hate being called a homosexual because I don't feel that way. It really upsets me. I particularly like working with children and motivating them, and we had a lot of ideas about programs for junior tennis. Now I think they're probably going to bag it and say, "I don't want this creep around my kids." I don't know why they bring this up when they talk about gay people, like they're all perverts who go after children. Being gay can happen in any walk of life, in any world. If you have one gay experience, does that mean you're gay? If you have one heterosexual experience, does that mean you're straight? Life doesn't work quite so cut and dried. With Marilyn, it's been over for a long, long time, since 1975 or 1976, but try to tell Marilyn that!

LK: Actually, when Billie Jean wasn't around, Marilyn and I got along famously. I would say that at some point in time I may have been jealous about Marilyn, but by and large, I never had any animosity towards her. I tried to help her out the best I could. Billie Jean and I seriously thought about divorce in 1973 or 1974, but neither one of us could get the energy up. I love Billie Jean and I would say that ultimately, if she could be happy then I would be happy. That may be too philosophical or too detached for most people, but that's how I feel. Love is not possession, it's caring for your mate and wanting her to be happy. It's not owning her or possessing her time necessarily. It's enjoying the relationship. I guess I'm different from most other people. I make Billie Jean angry sometimes because she'd like me to be more possessive. She'd like me to get mad.

BJK: No two people know when they marry how things are going to happen or how they're going to work out. You've got to be flexible. We're totally flexible. Larry and I have been through so much together, and that in itself can bind you.

LK: I think we're astounded that we're still married.

BJK: When Larry and I were in college [Cal. State, L.A.] and didn't have a dime between us, we used to just sit and talk about

our dreams for tennis. When you've had that kind of goal in your mind for years, you become driven when you finally have the opportunity to make it happen. We just killed ourselves. Our goals and dreams took over our whole lives. We paid a very big price to make it all happen. We gave up a lot of time together. He couldn't just be a tennis husband. But it was also very gratifying.

LK: Marilyn was Billie Jean's road manager for only a year and a half, but it was probably the most hectic time in both our lives. I was running three major businesses—*womenSports* magazine, World Team Tennis and WTT Properties—and publishing the league's programs and promoting three tournaments on the women's tour. I had an incredibly busy schedule which was very fulfilling for me but not so much for Billie Jean, who was running around the world playing tennis.

BJK: In 1973 there was the Bobby Riggs match, I was playing on the Virginia Slims tour and we founded the Women's Tennis Association at Wimbledon. I have never understood how we got through that time.

LK: Our marriage turned into something totally different from what I expected 16 years ago. When we were first married our goal was to settle down as soon as I got out of law school and have three kids and start a tennis team. In some ways Billie Jean and I are both disappointed. There are parts I'd like to remedy. When I got out of law school we should just have had a family. Once you opt out of that, anything could happen—and anything did happen. Billie Jean doesn't feel that she's gay, and she'd like to have a child if she can work it out.

BJK: If I want to have a baby, I better get this show on the road. Physically it's still possible. Didn't Yoko Ono have one when she was 42? I do like children, but I've been a career woman and that's one of the things career women have to deal with. I had to wait to have a career. The Virginia Slims circuit didn't start until I was 27. Larry and I are pioneers, and I think people have to realize that pioneers do go through more trying times. I don't like the word sacrifices. I made choices women now don't have to make. Whatever happens now, I still have my titles, my wins. That's one thing they can't take away from me. I may lose my endorsements but I still have me, my self-esteem, and I'll start over.

LK: And you still have me. I'll support you.

May 25, 1981

There were no clear winners in this bizarre palimony case. Barnett's lawsuit was dismissed but the scandal cost Billie Jean an estimated $500,000 a year in endorsements. In an ironic twist, the disputed Malibu beach house was destroyed in a coastal storm in 1983.

COUPLES

GRRRRACE

Disco singer Grace Jones
and French artist Jean-
Paul Goude often fought
like tigers, but the pair of
lovers managed to pro-
duce a son before their
fractious five years to-
gether ended in 1982.

CO RENTMEESTER

64

COUPLES

WIFELIKE FIGURE

Lee Marvin never kept Michelle Triola under wraps, letting her be called "Mrs. Marvin." She won (and later lost) only $104,000 but it was the principle of palimony that counted.

SPLITSMAN

"Within five years the marriage license won't matter," said divorce lawyer Marvin Mitchelson without a shred of doubt at a Vegas chapel in 1978.

Live-in lovers made grounds-breaking law as sweeties sued

For a number of the famous, the new *M Squad*—consisting of TV star Lee Marvin, his ex-live-in Michelle Triola and her lawyer Marvin Mitchelson—was about as welcome as the prospect of starring in *Gates of Heaven II*. Michelle

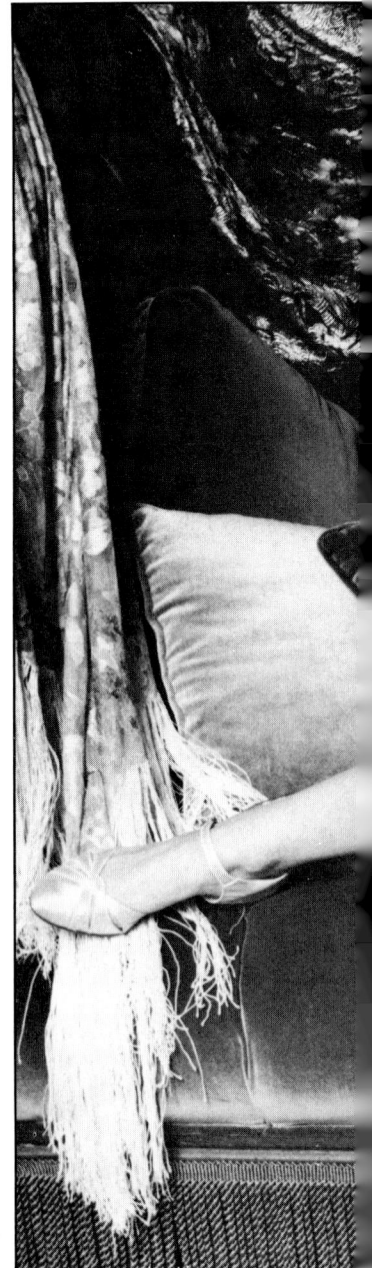

©1978 TONY KORODY/SYGMA

had lived with Lee, without matrimony although she adopted his last name, from 1964 to 1970, when he suddenly married old flame Pamela Feeley; then, in 1975, utilizing Hollywood's leading divorce attorney, Michelle sued Lee for $1.5 million, or roughly half his property from their years together. In 1976, a California court ruled she had grounds, and she was later awarded $104,000 "for rehabilitation purposes."

The sound of the gavel on that precedent-setting palimony case had hardly died away when model Cynthia Lang sued Vincent Furnier, a/k/a rocker Alice Cooper, for $5 million for their seven years together, with Mitchelson as her lawyer; actress Karen Louise Eklund sued Nick Nolte for $4.5 million for their five years, with Mitchelson at her side, too. Britt Ekland sued Rod Stewart for $15 million for their two years; and poor Flip Wilson got smacked twice—by ex-Playboy Bunny Rosylin Taylor for $375,000 plus half his assets from their 2½ years, and by dental assistant Kayatana Harrison for $135,000 for 1½ years. By 1979, more than a thousand cohabitation cases were lodged in California alone, and seven states had followed suit by legalizing roomies' rights.

Many of those cases were decided by judges, and a number of them exercised their prerogative to reverse each other's minds: In 1981, a California court of appeals overturned the financial award in the Marvin decision. But as Marvin ("I'm a feminist") Mitchelson noted, the courts let the principle of the case stand. "People no longer have to be licensed like pets to have rights," the palimony pioneer said. "Living together is itself an implied contract." Then he went out and set a U.S. record by winning a divorce settlement of $85 million for Italian beauty Sheika Dena Al-Fassi from her Saudi husband.

BRITT HAD GRIT

"We're the last of the great lovers, a contemporary Burton and Taylor," Britt Ekland once said, and when she sued Rod Stewart for $15 million, he got the point.

©STEVE SCHAPIRO

©JILL KREMENTZ

S-X TH---PY

"You look sexy," Dr. William Masters said to wife Virginia Johnson in her hat. He should know: M&J's pioneering books and two-week, $2,500 sex therapy sessions aided thousands.

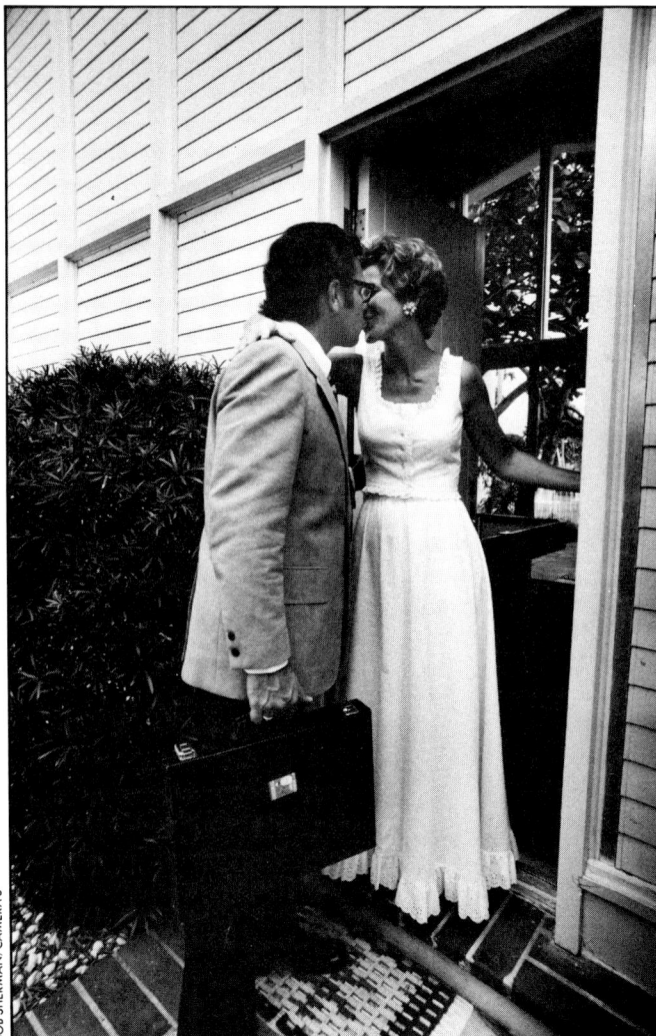

BOB SHERMAN/CAMERA 5

GETTING TOTALED

Marabel Morgan's motto in 1975 was "Let your husband be your master," and she taught her *Total Woman*hood to Anita Bryant, 12 Miami Dolphin wives and her own Charlie.

Four star generals in the battle of the sexes

What's a poor girl to do? In the early '70s that was a jocular rhetorical question but no more. With some 100 instructors in 28 states, *Total Woman-*izer Marabel Morgan, 37, exhorted such disparate listeners as Mrs. Joe Frazier and the Turkey Growers of America to let the male rule the roost; she herself, she confided, had greeted hubby Charlie in pink babydoll pj's and once had her way with him 'neath the dinner table by candlelight. In 1974 the solutions of sex therapists Dr. William Masters and Virginia Johnson were less simplistic: in books *(Human Sexual Response)* or counseling sessions, the once-divorced gynecologist and his four-times-married spouse put in 90-hour weeks helping couples shed their fears.

Her best-selling *Sex and the Single Girl* led Helen Gurley Brown to the editorship of *Cosmopolitan,* whence she italicized her way into the hearts of millions with zesty sexual confessionals and such gee-wheezes as "Marry a *nice* man." Too *dumb*? Consider that in 1982 the self-proclaimed flatterer, 60, and movie producer David Brown celebrated their 23rd anniversary. "Their marriage is all a fantasy," claimed one friend, but Helen demurred. "One thing I do quite well," she boasted, "is deal with reality."

MOUSEBURGER DE LUXE

Tiny, she said she was; drab, *shy,* figure *wrong,* a true *mouseburger.* So how come Helen Gurley snagged movie mogul David Brown (being bussed, center) and created that *Cosmo* Girl who attracted two million readers?

HARRY BENSON

69

STEPPIN' OUT WITH MY BABY

Jockey Robyn Smith, 38, retired for him and at 81 he hoofed "just for myself," but during their night and day marriage Fred Astaire showed (in 1981) that, even standing still, he simply reeked of class.

HARRY BENSON

On jogging paths and in gyms, at expensive spas and in their own backyards, Americans worked to trim down, tone up and take a stand against their newest wrinkle. With diet and exercise books dominating the best-seller lists, personal fitness went from a weekend pastime to a national obsession.

RICHARD FRANK ©1980

CO RENTMEESTER

MUSCLE AS ART

Arnold Schwarzenegger tensed his glutes for an audience of 2,500 at Manhattan's Whitney Museum of American Art in 1976, but Lisa Lyon, the first World Women's Bodybuilding Champion in 1979, demonstrated that a flex can be feminine as well.

BODY

BODY

SITTING PRETTY

With his gams pictured on 650,000 hardcover copies of *The Complete Book of Running,* author Jim Fixx in 1978 had the most celebrated legs since Betty Grable.

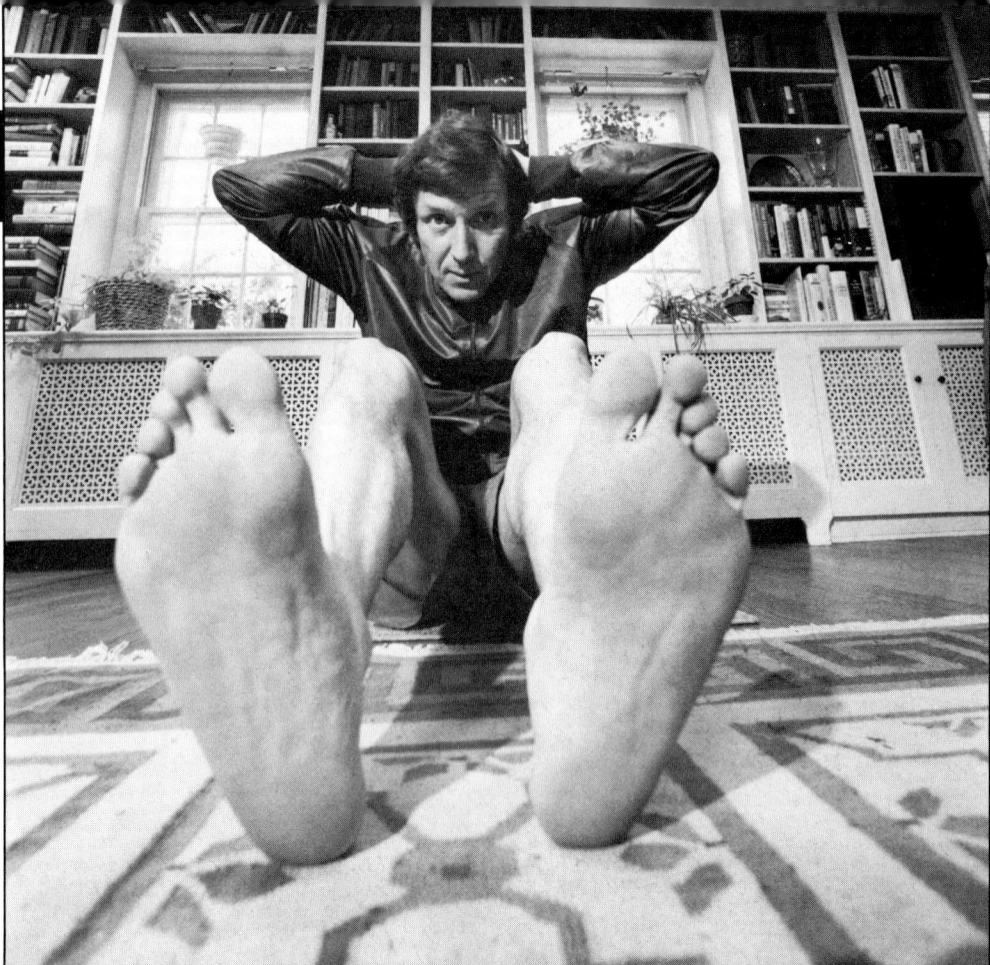

KEN REGAN/CAMERA 5

FIT AT 50

"No potion will make a woman my age young. But she can be beautiful," said Kaylan Pickford, whose middle-aged modeling career sparkled with champagne and diamond ads.

J. FREDERICK SMITH

JOHN DOMINIS

EVELYN FLORET

THE THIGHS HAVE IT

Wendy Stehling slimmed her stems with a diet and exercise program, then fattened her bank account with the 1982 best-seller, *Thin Thighs in 30 Days*.

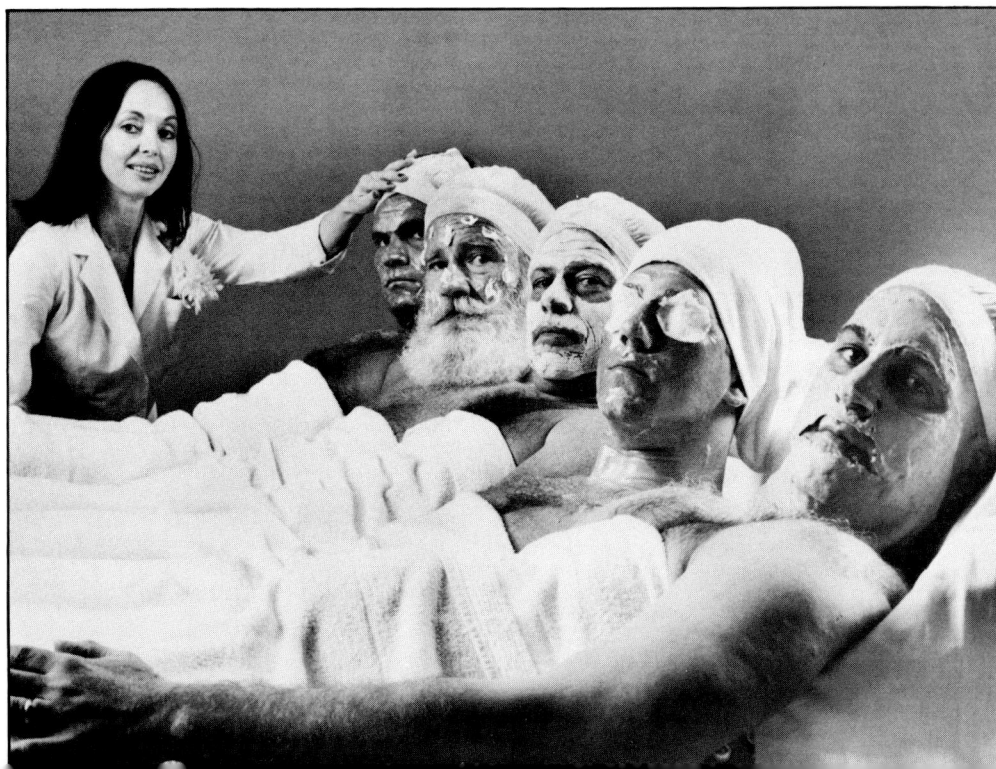

SAVING FACE

"In 10 years 50 percent of men will be wearing make-up, and I'll be there to save their skins," predicted cosmetologist Lia Schorr, who had 1,500 clients.

75

BODY

A Diet Doctor's Surprising Demise

To body-conscious calorie counters, few diet gurus have carried as much weight as Dr. Herman Tarnower. When PEOPLE profiled the 69-year-old cardiologist in June 1979, his *Complete Scarsdale Medical Diet* had already topped the hardcover best-seller lists for 10 weeks, and converts to his high-protein, low-carbohydrate regimen included House Speaker Tip O'Neill, *Ms.* editor Gloria Steinem and NBC newscaster Jane Pauley. Tarnower's program, originally devised as a guide for his own patients, prescribed a strict two-week menu and forbade alcohol, oils and sugar. Despite the spartan overtones, even Britain's Queen Elizabeth was rumored for a time to be devaluing her pounds the Scarsdale way.

Within months, however, Tarnower's success was suddenly overshadowed by lurid scandal when, on March 10, 1980, the famed physician was shot to death in the bedroom of his rambling country home in Purchase, N.Y. Charged with his killing was Jean Harris, 57, headmistress of the exclusive Madeira School for girls in Greenway, Va. A longtime lover and confidante of the bachelor doctor (Harris had been cited in the diet book's acknowledgments "for her splendid assistance in the research and writing"), she insisted on her innocence and that the four gunshot wounds were accidental.

In the turbulent trial that followed, prosecutors depicted Harris as a scorned woman jealous over Tarnower's dalliance with Lynne Tryforos, an aide 32 years his junior. Convicted of second degree murder, Harris was given a 15-year-to-life sentence and was sent to serve her time at the Bedford Hills Correctional Facility in Westchester County, N.Y.

BEFORE THE FALL

Lynne Tryforos, shown with Tarnower in an outtake from PEOPLE's original photo session, eventually emerged as a principal in the deadly love triangle.

ARTHUR SCHATZ

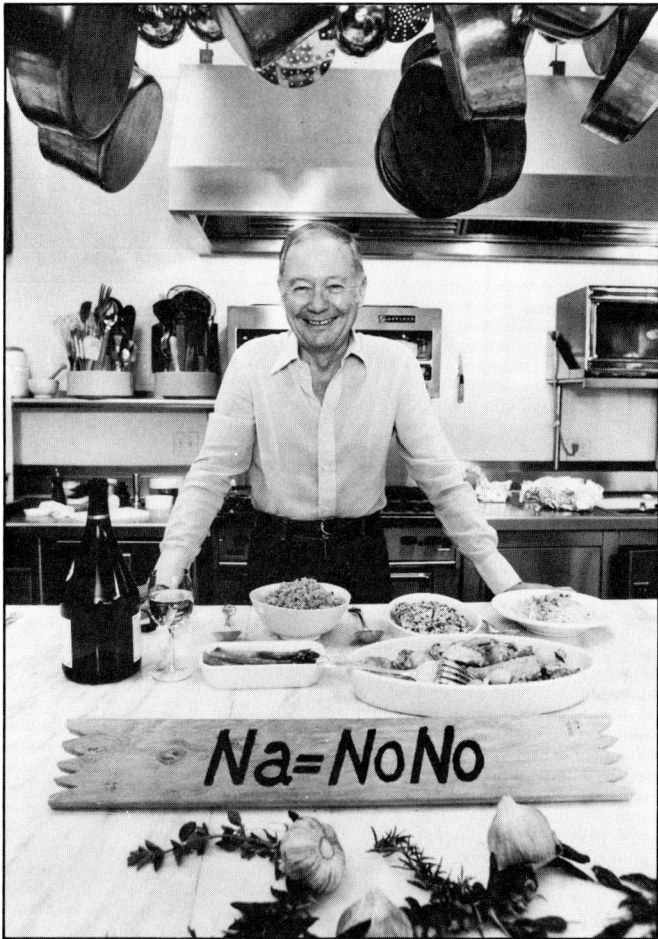

SHAKING SALT

Alarmed by his high blood pressure, *New York Times* food critic Craig Claiborne switched to a diet low in sodium (Na) and made the most of it by writing a new cookbook.

ARTHUR SCHATZ

RAEANNE RUBENSTEIN

ROOM FOR TWO

James Coco, shown sharing his old pair of pants with a pal, shed 110 pounds with a 700-calorie-a-day diet and therapy.

RAEANNE RUBENSTEIN

SHOWING STARCH

"It settles your tummy and warms your insides," said culinary big cheese James Beard, author of a 1983 book on pasta.

BODY

HANGING OUT

Folks flipped for Dr. Robert Martin (with tie) and the Inversion Boots he claimed could cure back pain and other ailments.

LOW-CAL CAMP

Richard Simmons used a carrot and shtik approach on his TV fitness program and became known as America's sultan of svelte.

FLEXIBLE FONDA

Strong as ever at the box office, the actress turned hot-selling author with the aerobics-oriented *Jane Fonda's Workout Book.*

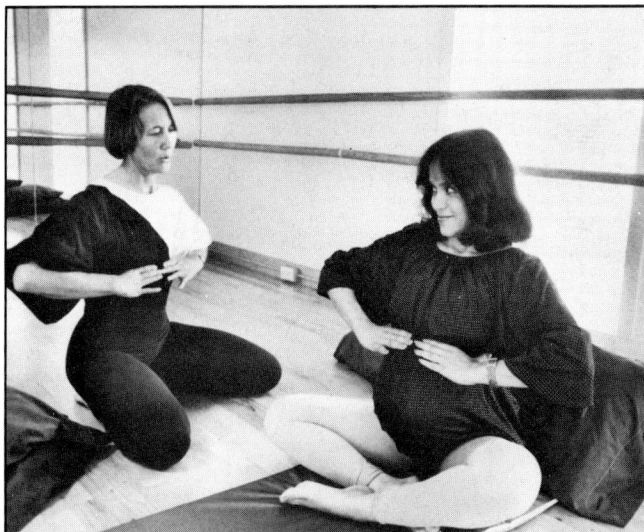

HARRY BENSON

SHAPING UP MOM

Childbirth expert Femmy De Lyser (left) kept Fonda fit during her second pregnancy, then worked out a regimen for mothers-to-be at Jane's Beverly Hills exercise studio.

MARK SENNET/SHOOTING STAR

BODY

ON THE ROAD

Calling his jogs "a type of meditation," former California Governor Jerry Brown logged up to 50 miles per week. However, his 1982 run for the Senate came up short.

HEALTHY BALANCE

Once a childhood victim of rheumatic fever, actor Roy Scheider toughened up with his thrice-weekly gymnastics workouts.

JOHN OLSON

**CORPUS
DELECTABLE**

Dallas actress Victoria Principal had the bod most envied by other women according to the 1983 poll of PEOPLE readers.

TEACHERS & HEALERS

Whether with those ministering to the poor in Calcutta or with skilled surgeons on the attack in the operating room, PEOPLE has been an inquiring witness. Here are the menders of body and soul, the tenders of the mind who have brought their special gifts to the world.

ZEN GETAWAY

One of only six Zen masters in the United States in 1975, Eido Shimano oversaw creation of a Japanese-style retreat in upstate New York.

SIDEWALK SAINT

"Our work is for people who have forgotten how to smile," said Mother Teresa, whose labor with the sick and homeless of Calcutta earned her a 1979 Nobel Peace Prize.

TEACHERS & HEALERS

MASS APPEAL

Notre Dame President Theodore Hesburgh proved he could mix priestly chores with his duties as an outspoken adviser to Presidents Johnson, Nixon and Carter.

DOLLAR DAZE

Frederick Eikerenkoetter (a/k/a Rev. Ike) earned $250,000 a week for his ministry by preaching a pie-in-the-sky-now brand of positive thinking.

GLASS HOUSE OF GOD

California/TV evangelist Robert Schuller's Crystal Cathedral cost $18 million; charging up to $150 for pop concerts there cost the Reverend its tax-exempt status.

TEACHERS & HEALERS

ARTHUR GRACE

SWINGING LOW

University of Illinois classics prof Richard Scanlan, who used showbiz theatrics to make his courses big on campus, showed up in style at a 1978 homecoming rally.

CHIEF CLIFFIE

Psychologist Matina Horner didn't let motherhood (three kids) hold her back when, at 32, she became Radcliffe College's youngest president.

DALE WITTNER

MODERN MR. CHIPS

Troubled kids found discipline, therapy and homey warmth at Michael DeSisto's school in Massachusetts. In 1981, 90 percent headed for college.

BACK TO BASICS

Larry Olsen's survival course in 1977 featured 10 days in the Montana wilds with only a change of clothes, blanket and pocketknife for protection.

CENTER STAGE

New Mexico drama teacher Mark Medoff won campus kudos when his Broadway play, *Children of a Lesser God,* copped a 1980 Tony award.

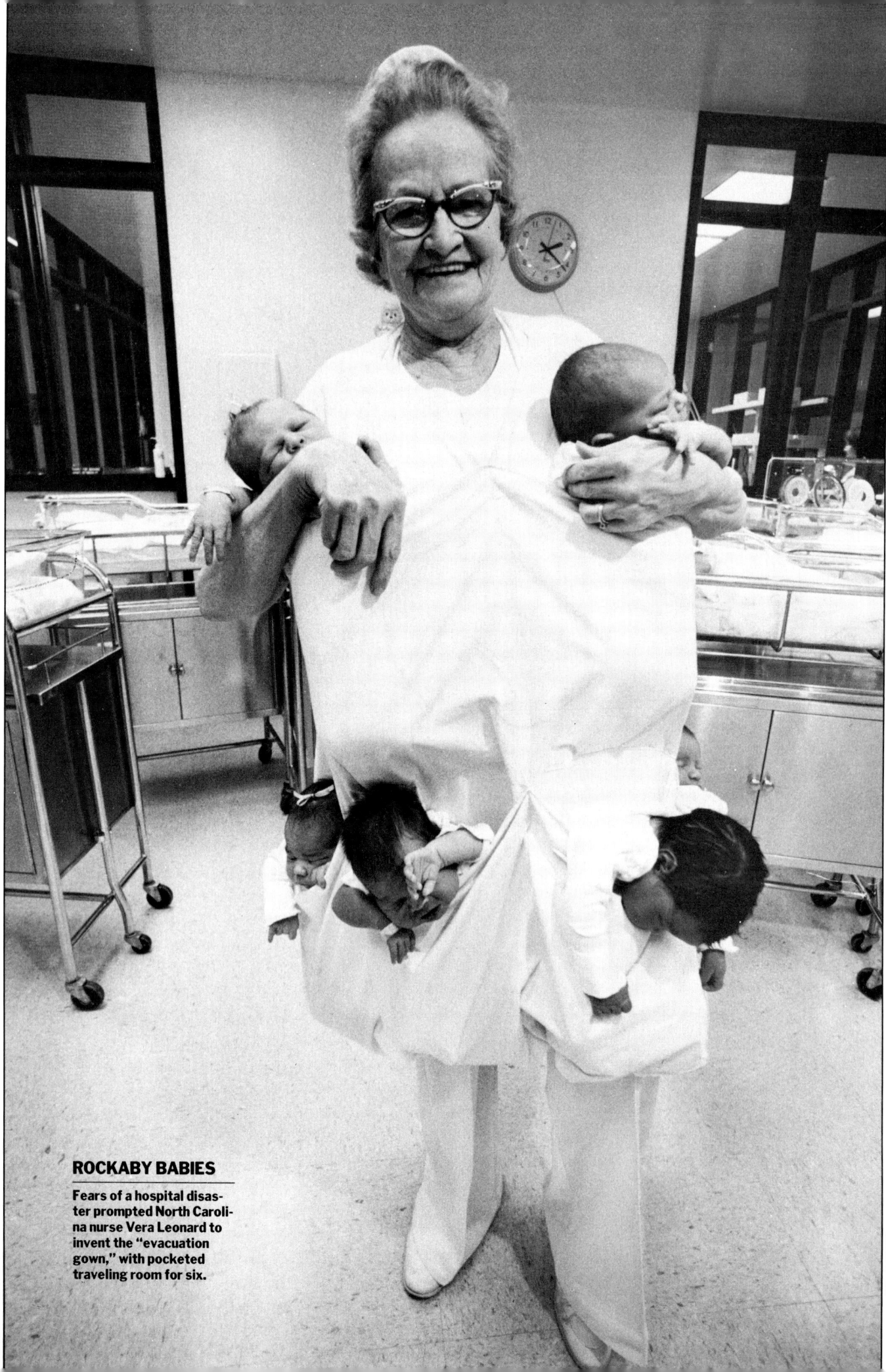

ROCKABY BABIES

Fears of a hospital disaster prompted North Carolina nurse Vera Leonard to invent the "evacuation gown," with pocketed traveling room for six.

TEACHERS
&HEALERS

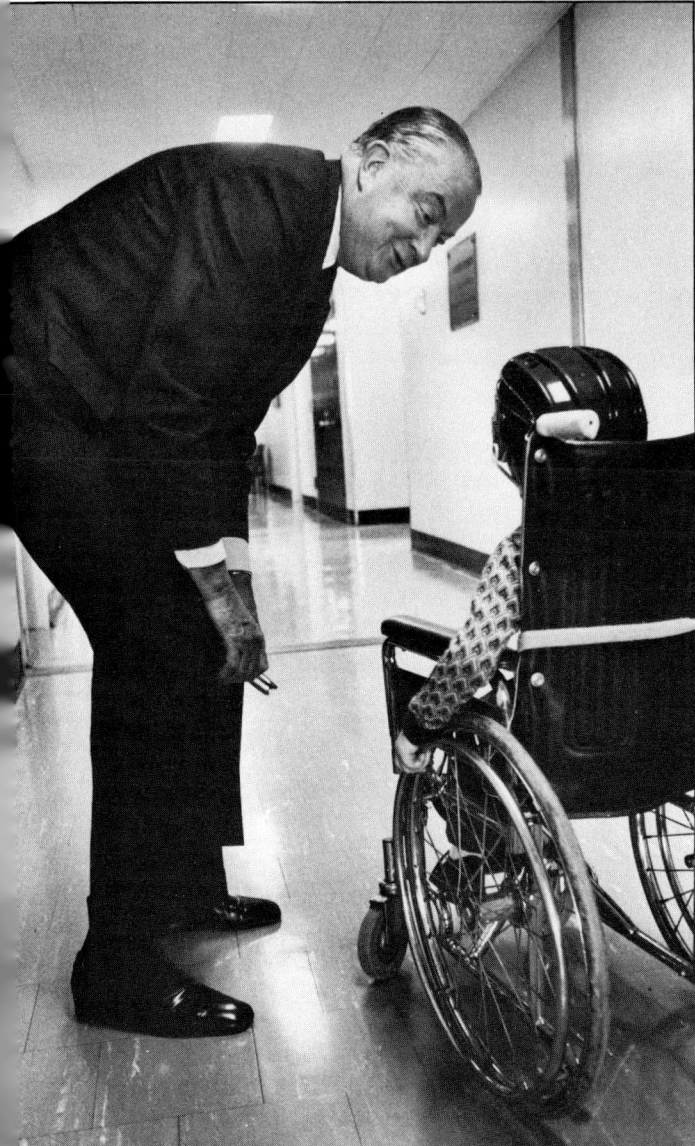

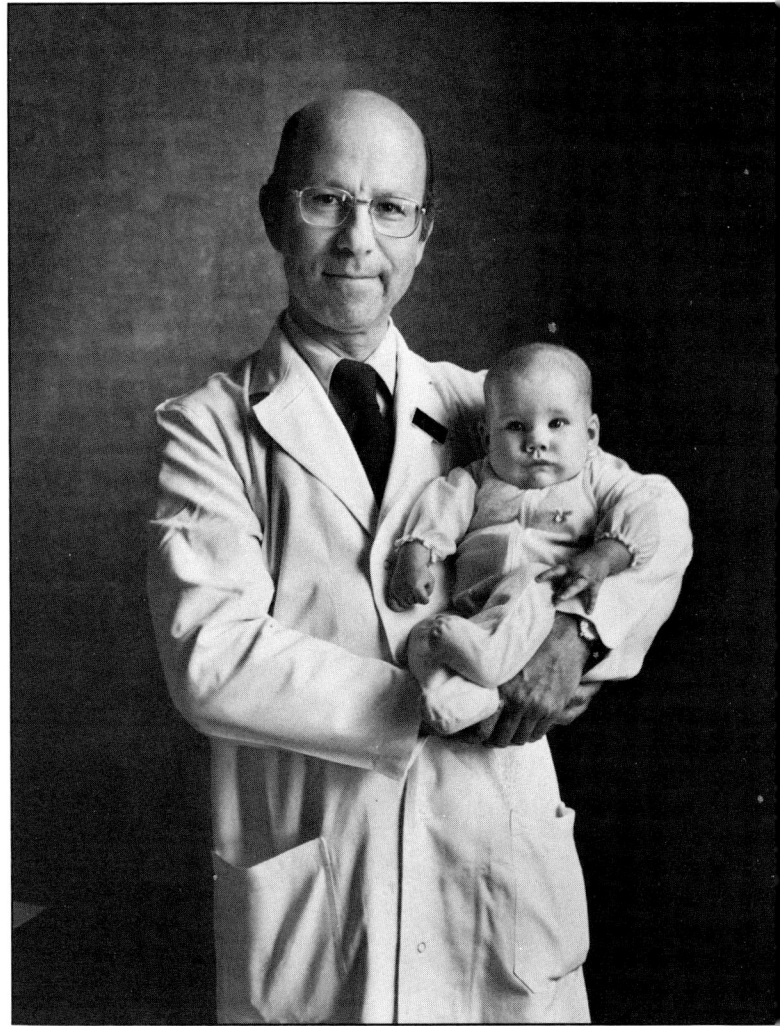

KID TALK

His brother, Jonas, licked polio, but New York child psychologist Lee Salk made a name for himself with his book, *What Every Child Would Like His Parents to Know.*

REHAB MASTER

A boy wearing a protective helmet against falls got a personal look-see from Dr. Howard Rusk of New York's famed Institute of Rehabilitation Medicine in 1976.

89

TEACHERS
& HEALERS

ORGAN MAKERS

Artificial kidney machine inventor Willem Kolff in 1975 examined a pioneering model of a plastic heart built by then third year medical student Robert Jarvik.

©MICHAEL ALEXANDER 1983

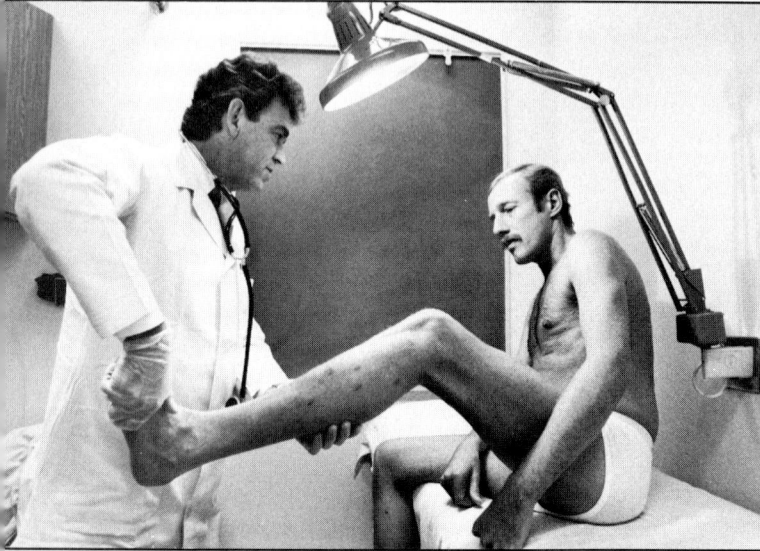

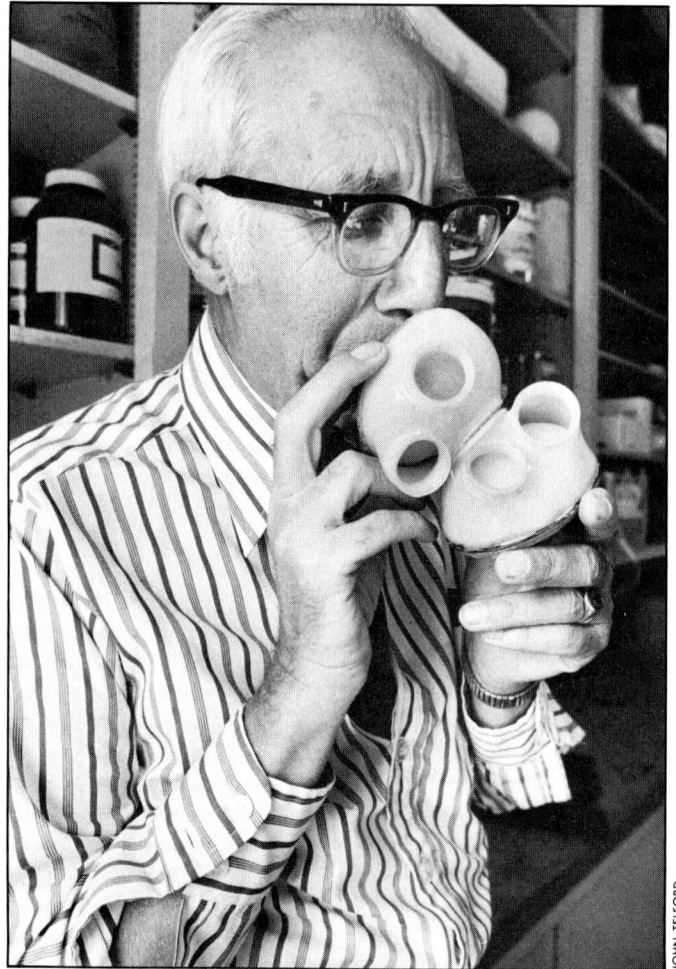

JOHN TELFORD

AIDS ONSLAUGHT

San Francisco's Dr. Marcus Conant examined Oscar Romig for Kaposi's sarcoma in 1983 as acquired immune deficiency syndrome (AIDS), which makes victims prey to disease, spread.

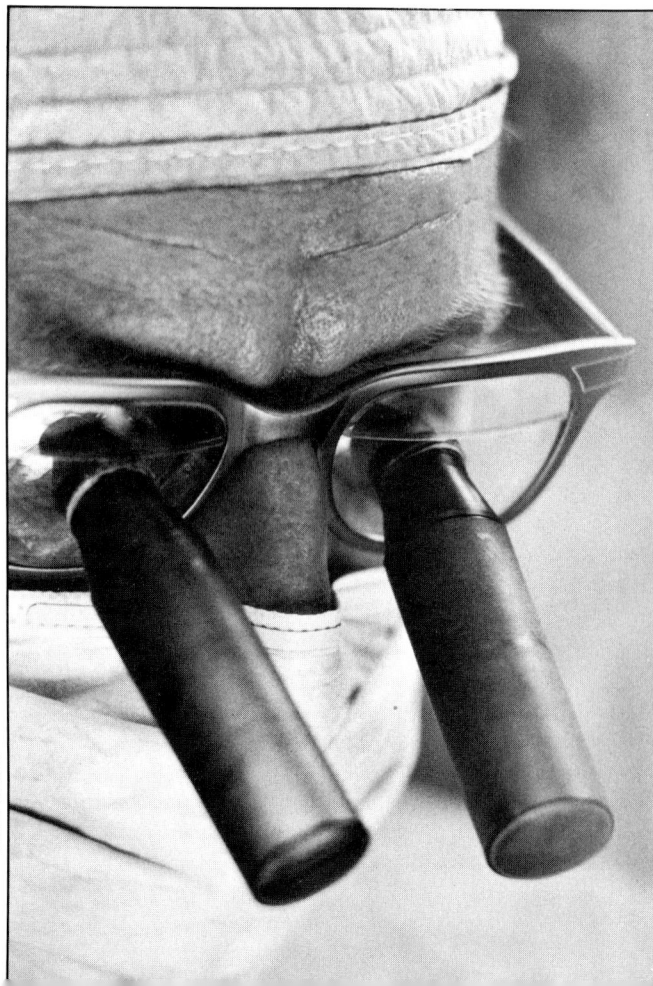

FINE WORK

"It's kind of like fixing a watch," said Dr. Harold Kleinert of the microsurgery he helped develop that permits the reattachment of severed limbs.

WILLIAM STRODE

ACE OF HEARTS

Utah's Dr. William DeVries implanted a Jarvik artificial heart in ailing Seattle dentist Barney Clark in 1982. The courageous patient survived 112 days.

WEIGHTY CONCERNS

Dr. Tom Starzl (second from right), who in 1963 became the first to transplant a human liver, hefted a donor's organ before surgery in 1978.

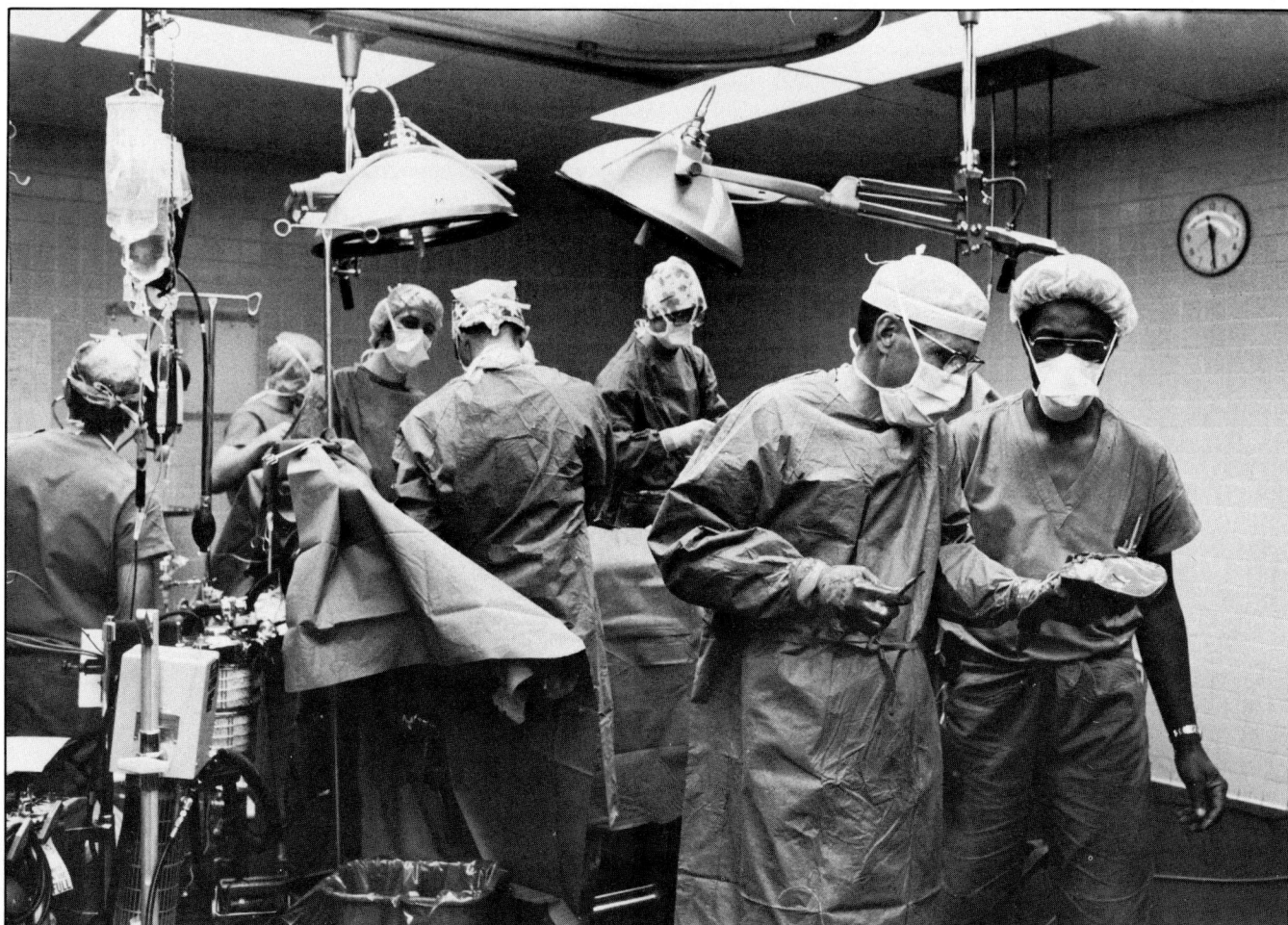

Style

From Paris and Milan to Seventh Avenue, fashion thrived, clothes makers turned into cult figures, and mannequins and blue-jeaned babies became media stars.

BOTTOM LINES

While heiress-designer Gloria Vanderbilt slapped her name on the hip pockets of the hoi polloi, Bronx-born Calvin Klein and his sweet-16 pitch girl, Brooke Shields, mounted their own campaign to denim America's derrieres.

EVELYN FLORET

CO RENTMEESTER

Style

DANIEL BOUDINET

COUNT KARL

"I'm sort of a vampire, taking the blood of other people," said designer Karl Lagerfeld in 1975, citing some of the sources (including '30s movies) from which he borrowed.

SAINT YVES

After the 1974 showing of his fall couture collection in Paris, shy designer Yves Saint Laurent (far right) got a hand from press and pals like Catherine Deneuve (center).

95

Style

DESIGNS ON THE WEST

Tight clothes on women "don't look noble," protested Japan's Yohji Yamamoto, whose ready-to-wear styles translated into big U.S. sales.

GOING WITH THE FLOW

Milan's Giorgio Armani struck gold with his loose, unstructured look in men's clothing, then cut out a luxurious piece of the women's wear market.

YOSHIHIKO UEDA

96

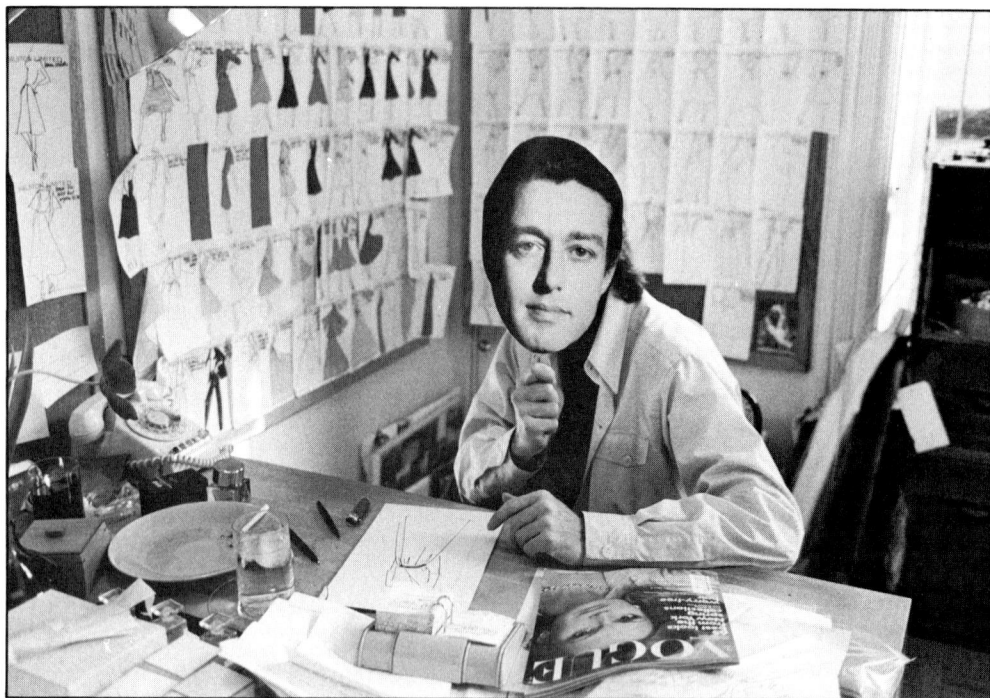

Style

© JILL KREMENTZ

FACE OF SUCCESS

"A designer is only as good as his clientele," decreed Halston, whose satisfied customers included Jackie O, Liz Taylor and Liza Minnelli.

©STEVE SCHAPIRO

KING OF GLITZ

Bob Mackie (with partner Ray Aghayan, right) covered the busiest bods in show business with feathers, sequins and high-priced finery.

HANN
RROLL

AROL
RNETT

ANN-MARGRET

SIREN OF SEVENTH AVE.

"I think a woman should dress for men," advised designer-businesswoman Diane von Furstenberg, who often seemed her firm's best advertisement.

Style

BEASTLY BUSY

Supermodel Cheryl Tiegs padded her portfolio with a $2.5 million ABC-TV contract that took her to Africa in 1978 with photographer Peter Beard. At home she promoted her line of clothes for Sears.

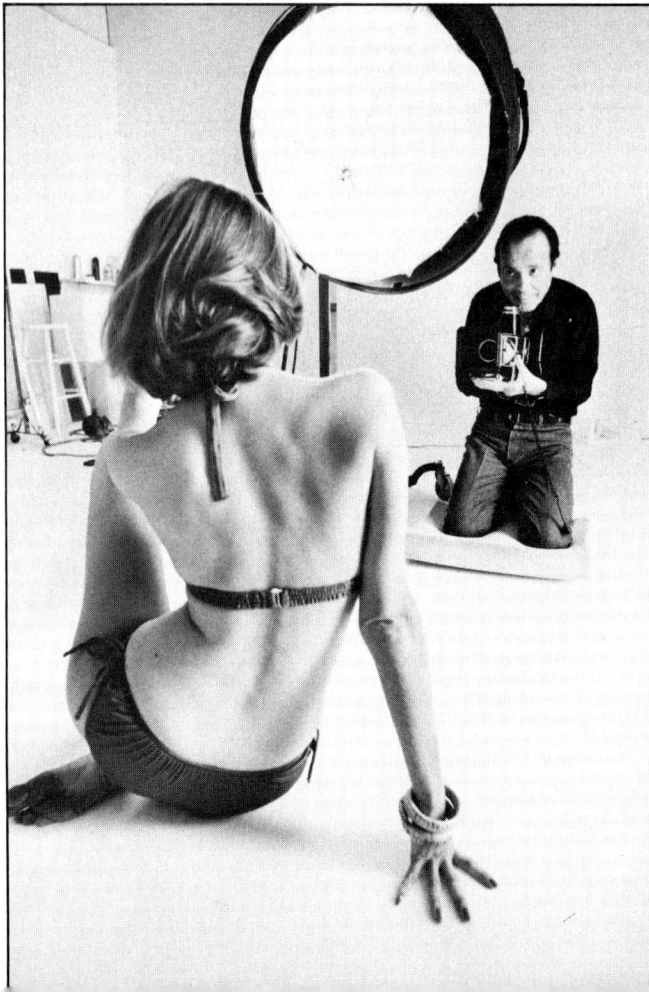

BEST SHOT

"Making women look their best is what I like to do," summed up famed fashion photographer Francesco Scavullo, here working his camera magic with model Melanie Cain.

DAY WORK

Despite her 200 magazine covers and $2,500-a-day fees, Christie Brinkley said, "Modeling is a 9-to-5 business with me. I don't take it seriously."

ARTHUR SCHATZ

MEGA celebs

Frothy hair
might do it, or a really
great smile. Talent helps.
Youth isn't required but some sexiness
is, originality is a must, and somehow they make an impact beyond their
work without worrying too much about
what anybody thinks. By whatever magic, some few put an indelible
mark on each decade, and these
people left their stamp
on our time.

FARRAH FAWCETT

Remember the teeth? The poster? The T-shirt? The jiggle?
They spelled the giddiest
overnight smash in decades.
A few years later she was off
Charlie's Angels—"I was
surprised I was so easy to
replace"—with a string of
middling movies, mending
her image off-Broadway.
But who else was, for three
resplendent years, the world's
most sought-after woman?

103

MEGA celebs

DIANA, PRINCESS OF WALES

Her eyes down modestly, her cheeks blushing the color of an English tea rose, her smile delighted as a child's, a 19-year-old kindergarten teacher burst on the world in 1981 as though conjured out of air, and the world was smitten. As the daughter of Lord Spencer and thus a lady to the manor born, she grew up calling the Queen "Aunt Lilibet." Shy Di sailed triumphantly through a wedding to her future king. Then she gave her countrymen Prince William, and so they kept calling to her: "You're beautiful, luv."

MUHAMMAD ALI

A man terrified, the pre-fight
doctor called him, the day in
1964 he whupped Liston in the
seventh and became champ,
but the word surely should
have been "transported."
Years later Father Time
caught up with the butterfly
and the bee, but not too early.
By then, bragging, rhyming,
jiving, The Greatest had
knocked everybody out.

MIKHAIL BARYSHNIKOV

Moody, complex, he is a zesty
chameleon of all styles on
stage—"more caring about
his partner than himself," said
one—and his Emmy-winning
TV tribute to Broadway shone
with the delight of a master
fan. Seven years after defect-
ing, he fathered a daughter
by Oscar-winning actress
Jessica Lange; at the American Ballet Theatre his baby
ballerinas brightened
all ballet.

DINA MAKAROVA

BROOKE
SHIELDS

She got these sapphires from a *sheik* plus diamonds from his *son* plus 1,000 birthday balloons from a *prince* plus *zillions* for modeling and acting, kind of, in movies—and know what she loved best? Mocha chip ice cream! She has tons of hair, really *blue* eyes and teased the entire *universe* with her *Mom* watching! Un*real*!

JOHN BRYSON

ELIZABETH
TAYLOR

The indefinable something that made her a star at 12 had clearly grown during seven marriages, two Oscars and five near-fatal illnesses, but by the mid-'70s, billed second to her Senator-spouse, she was dubbed "QE3" and seemed beached. So in 1981, at 49, she shed 40 pounds, made Broadway swoon in *The Little Foxes*, followed up opposite Hubby Five and Six, Richard Burton, with an SRO production of *Private Lives*. That's showin' 'em, Liz.

DUSTIN
HOFFMAN

As a kid, he "was never looked at." Now, wherever the societal action is, there you'll see him. He's been a seduced naif in *The Graduate*, a pimp (*Midnight Cowboy*), a reporter (*All the President's Men*), a single papa (*Kramer*) and a man gorgeously faking it as a gutsy dame—modeled on his mom—in *Tootsie*. For it he got $4.5 million-plus. Who says there's no justice!

RAEANNE RUBENSTEIN

111

MEGA
celebs

RON GALELLA

JACQUELINE ONASSIS

No one has been more photographed, more written about and less known. Twenty years after she became a widow and ceased being First Lady, nine years after being widowed by Ari Onassis, she is still beautiful, a mother, an editor, rides, dates, supports causes and owns a summer place with decks of teak on Martha's Vineyard. And, she might smile, "That is all ye need to know."

CHER

As a '60s singer, she didn't so much rise above dumb songs as yank them up to her. She was also the first hippie siren, making the nutty, slinky, peek-a-boo gowns she loved seem immaterial—they nearly were—and sex just so much kitschy-coo. She hasn't kept a last name long, despite repeated tries, but she bewitched playgoers on first try. "I have a *lot* of nerve," said she. Yeah, and hooray.

DIANA ROSS

The rock explosion of the '60s didn't leave many on the shore afterwards, but there she was. *Wiz* director Sidney Lumet called her "a supernova exploding," and to play Dorothy she marked *Oz* passages in Day-Glo pink. She turns heads with her glitzy chic, can break a heart with one note, loved both Studio 54 and Kipling's *If*. After 23 years, the scene is still with the cream of the Supremes.

MICK JAGGER

One moment, back when the Stones first mixed shock and shimmy, he said he'd sooner be dead than singing *Satisfaction* after 40. The next moment it was '81, he was pushing 40, and they were in the throes of a 15-state (including Euphoria) U.S. tour, shooting truancy in some schools up to 20 percent. The Rolling Stones simply have defined their times, all 22 years, and there's *Still Life* in the old boys yet.

MEGA celebs

BARBRA STREISAND

She's touchy, shy, suspicious, pushy, abrasive, driven, spoiled, homely and is missing a letter in one name. True, she's also street-smart, classy, sassy, honest, alluring and a goofy bombshell with a riveting singing and acting style; plus she has Grammys, an Emmy, a Tony, two Oscars and her first directing credit. "The best description," said Kris Kristofferson, "is 'formidable.'"

JOANNE WOODWARD and PAUL NEWMAN

Her old man, the sex symbol, actor, director and car racer, has gone from *The Hustler, Hud, Butch Cassidy* and *The Sting* to *The Verdict* without accepting "the rubbish of Hollywood"—or winning an Oscar. His old lady, the sensible homemaker, has gone from an Oscar for her first lead to stage acting, directing and operating a 52-acre horse farm. Two staying powers.

HARRY BENSON

LENA HORNE

It took time but she finally turned spunk, flair, fortune and misfortune into a number all her own. First a "chocolate chanteuse," she was by 30 "a good little symbol" in Hollywood, where they darkened her fair negritude with Light Egyptian makeup; by 40, her bitterness showed. But, at 64, a widowed grandma with storms weathered, she ruled Broadway solo with all her heart and soul. Keeps reigning all the time.

HARRY BENSON

MEGA
celebs

PAUL McCARTNEY

Married back in 1969, father to four small fry and with a fortune estimated at $440 million, he was the Beatles' best balladeer. His later band, Wings, kept sweeping down on the pop camp like musical marauders and, in 1982, abetted by Stevie Wonder, it held the top spot with *Ebony and Ivory* for seven weeks. Some party when the music never stops.

ROBERT REDFORD

It was an offbeat bio for Hollywood's top draw: rancher, horse breeder, wilderness owner, solar energy advocate, ski resort builder, pilot, director, family sort, worrier about fame, and sewer commissioner of Provo Canyon, Utah. He shed the pressure by riding alone. "I don't think I'll ever be able to watch myself comfortably," he said. Which was odd; most others could.

RICHARD PRYOR

Brought up in his grandma's brothel, he moved on to stealing and brawling, and nearly died of third-degree burns when the coke and alcohol he was free-basing went up. Doesn't *sound* funny but on screen and records (five Grammys) his cheery conspiratorial air made him a soul brother under just about every skin.

BRUCE W. TALAMON

MEGA
celebs

JOHNNY CARSON

He would bestride the entertainment world like a colossus if he weren't sitting most of the time. With his fuddled stare, he is part cosmopolite, part wily bumpkin; no one makes the same hay out of disasters in a monologue; and after 22 years, he was to his 12 million viewers just what he always wanted to be, a magician: It's still impossible to see how he does it.

124

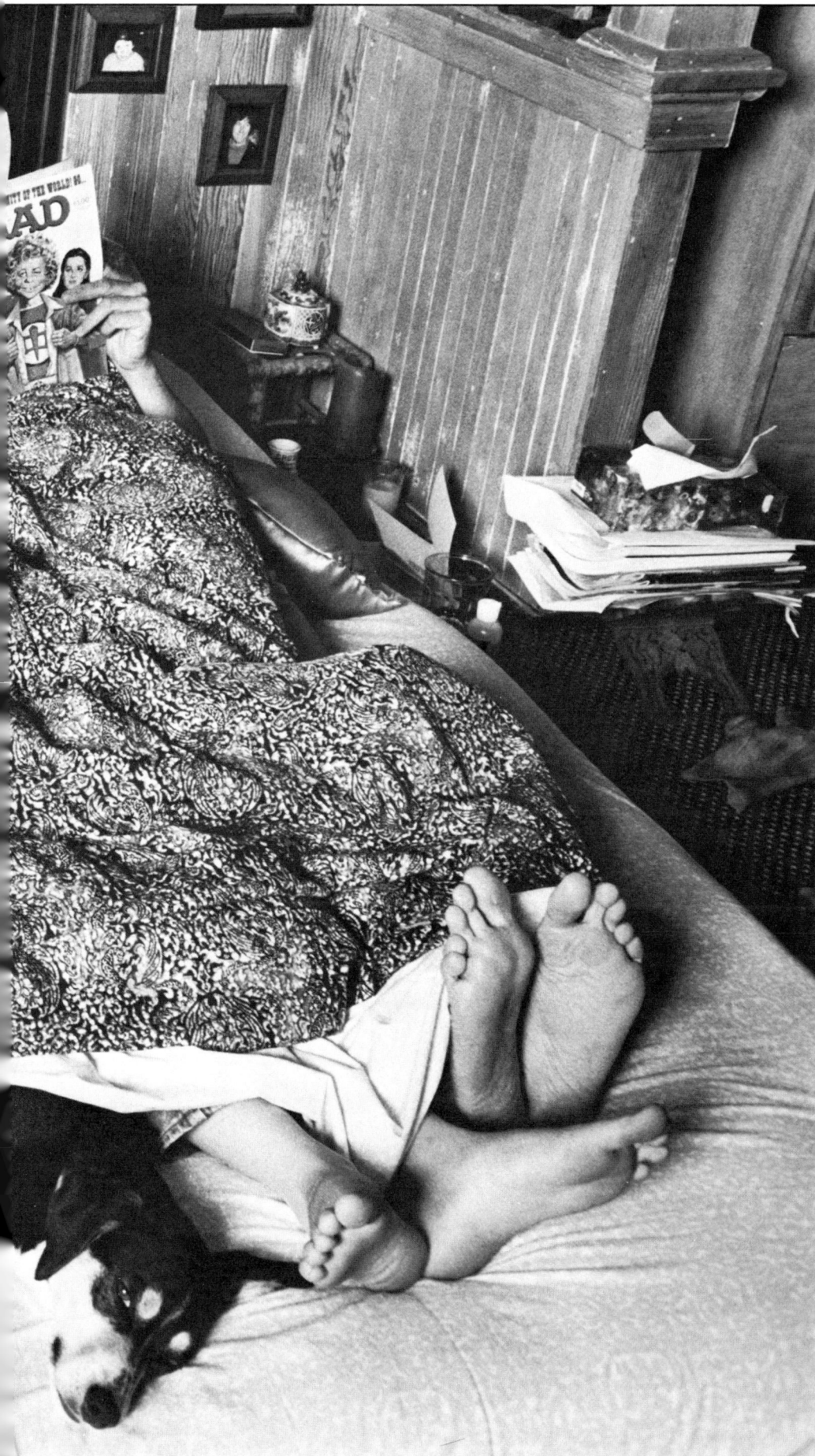

JANE
FONDA

How many people can you count in the bed? There's the sexy starlet of *Barbarella*; the ex-wife of Roger Vadim; the Vietnam era's "Hanoi Jane"; a double Oscar winner (*Klute, Coming Home*); wife of California assemblyman Tom Hayden; mother of two (see feet); a movie producer (*9 to 5, On Golden Pond*); and a tycoon with two fitness best-sellers and salons which were luring 10,000 customers a week. "These days," she said in 1982 at 44, "I'm almost mainstream." Welcome to the neighborhood, gang.

COVERS

The first face to greet PEOPLE readers each week is the cover portrait, influencing whether they buy the magazine at the newsstand or checkout counter. Quite naturally, the choice of cover subjects engrosses the editors' attention. And so, early on, managing editor Richard Stolley arrived at Stolley's Cover Law:

"Young is better than old, Pretty is better than ugly, Television is better than music, Music is better than movies, Movies are better than sports, And anything is better than politics."

Indeed PEOPLE's worst-selling issues do include prominent political figures such as Ted Kennedy Sr.

(1974), Nancy and Ronald Reagan (1976) and Vice President Mondale (1978). Jocks too took tumbles, with both Larry Csonka (1974) and Bjorn Borg (1977) low men. The law is not immutable; songsters also scraped the bottom.

What about the editors' favorites, those who appeared most often on the cover? Britain's Lady Di (now Princess of Wales) and Hollywood's Liz Taylor topped the list, followed by Jane Fonda, Brooke Shields and John Travolta, trailed by a crowded field that included Jacqueline Onassis, Cher, Farrah Fawcett, Goldie Hawn, Barbra Streisand, Burt Reynolds, Robert Redford and Warren Beatty.

IN THIS ISSUE

William Peter Blatty
'The Exorcist': "A sermon nobody sleeps through"

Marina Oswald
Finally at peace with herself

Gloria Vanderbilt
A fourth marriage that really works

Solzhenitsyn
From his own writing: A chilling account of a good man's arrest

Stephen Burrows
Fashion king of the sexy cling

The Loud Family
Broken up, but closer than ever

Palm Beach Whirl
The parties, pets and personalities

Vietnam MIA Wives
Demanding answers that nobody has

Jim Croce
Million-dollar music legacy

Richard Petty
Daredevil at Daytona

The Hearsts
During the nightmare

People Puzzle

People weekly — March 4, 1974 — 35 Cents

Mia Farrow
In 'Gatsby,' the year's next big movie

VOL. 1, NO. 1: MIA FARROW

ON THE COVER

Telly Savalas
He made 'Kojak' the No. 1 show

Bridget & Bernie
Now married for real

Cesar Chavez
A nonviolent man in the fight of his life

The Minibikini
Less is more

Margaret Trudeau
A nursing mother on the campaign trail

Charlie Quarry
The blonde in her husband's corner

People weekly — 35¢ — 1974

TELLY SAVALAS: THE FIRST MILLION-COPY SALE

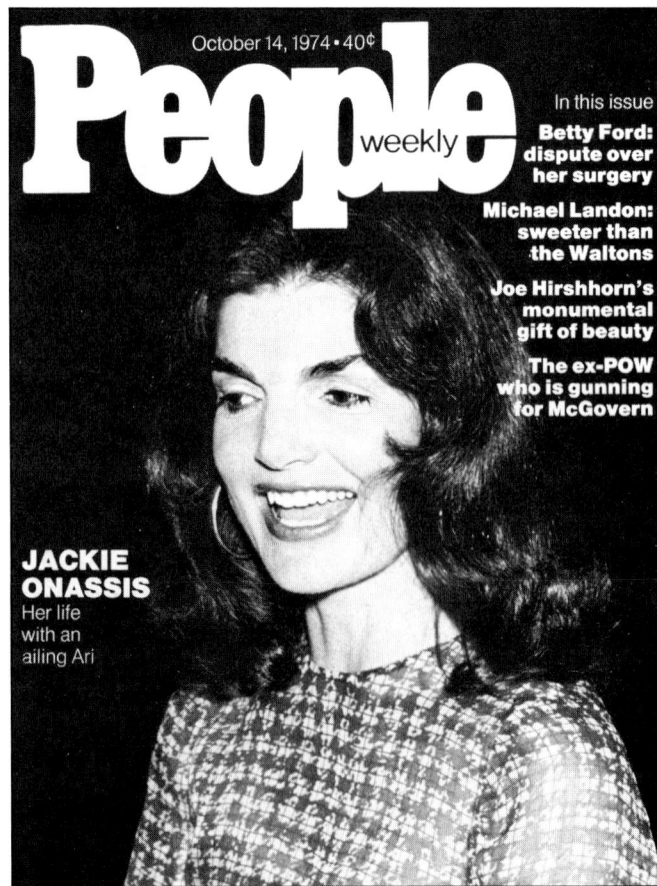

People weekly — October 14, 1974 • 40¢

In this issue

Betty Ford: dispute over her surgery

Michael Landon: sweeter than the Waltons

Joe Hirshhorn's monumental gift of beauty

The ex-POW who is gunning for McGovern

JACKIE ONASSIS
Her life with an ailing Ari

JACKIE ONASSIS: 1974'S NO. 2 BEST-SELLER

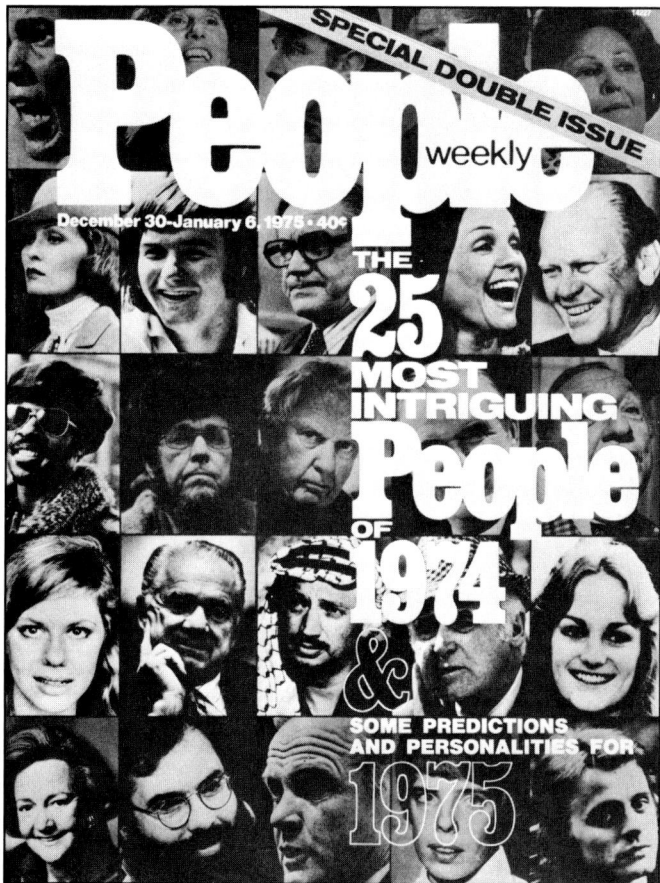

1974'S LAST ISSUE WAS THE FIRST DOUBLE ISSUE

1975 BEST-SELLER

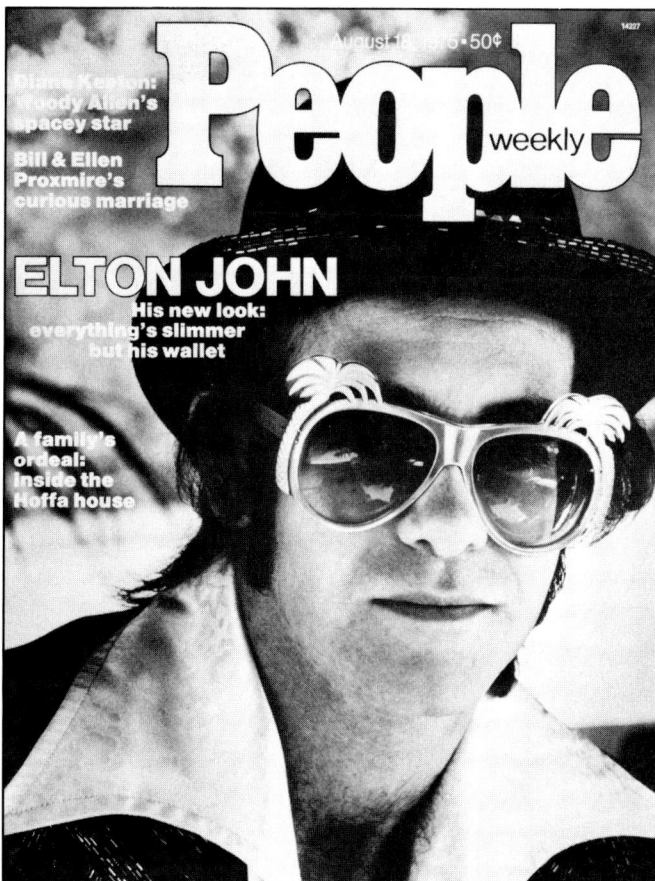

1975 RUNNER-UP

1976 BEST-SELLER

COVERS

December 6, 1976 • 50¢

Bardot, the new name in labels

Bill Bradley, cerebral jock

Picasso's widow ends mourning a multimillionaire

Charlie's Angels

How three sweet Southern girls became TV's hit team

1976 RUNNER-UP

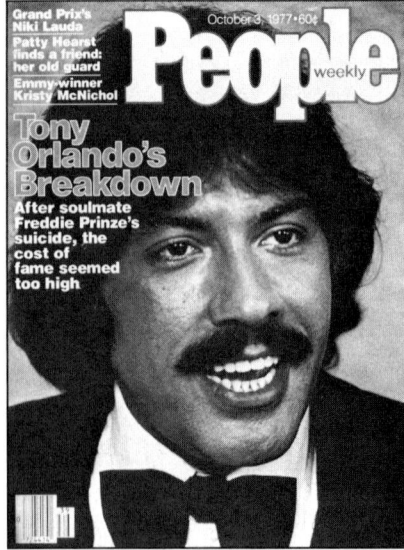

Grand Prix's Niki Lauda

Patty Hearst finds a friend: her old guard

Emmy-winner Kristy McNichol

October 3, 1977 • 60¢

Tony Orlando's Breakdown

After soulmate Freddie Prinze's suicide, the cost of fame seemed too high

1977 BEST-SELLER

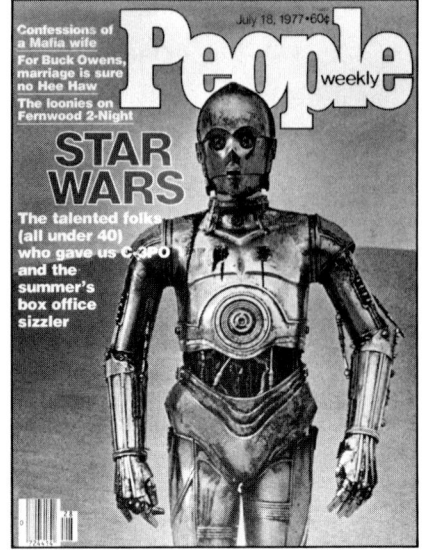

Confessions of a Mafia wife

For Buck Owens, marriage is sure no Hee Haw

The loonies on Fernwood 2-Night

July 18, 1977 • 60¢

STAR WARS

The talented folks (all under 40) who gave us C-3PO and the summer's box office sizzler

1977 RUNNER-UP

Massacre in Guyana: why it happened

Love on the set of 'All My Children'

Barbara Walters remembers her impresario Dad

A bartender makes it in pro football

DECEMBER 4, 1978 • 75¢

PRISCILLA PRESLEY

Elvis' ex-wife talks about their marriage, their daughter, his death & her new career

1978 BEST-SELLER

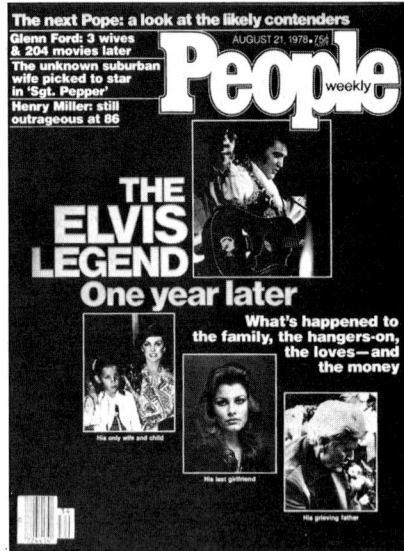

The next Pope: a look at the likely contenders

Glenn Ford: 3 wives & 204 movies later

The unknown suburban wife picked to star in 'Sgt. Pepper'

Henry Miller: still outrageous at 86

AUGUST 21, 1978 • 75¢

THE ELVIS LEGEND

One year later

What's happened to the family, the hangers-on, the loves—and the money

His only wife and child

His last girlfriend

His grieving father

1978 RUNNER-UP

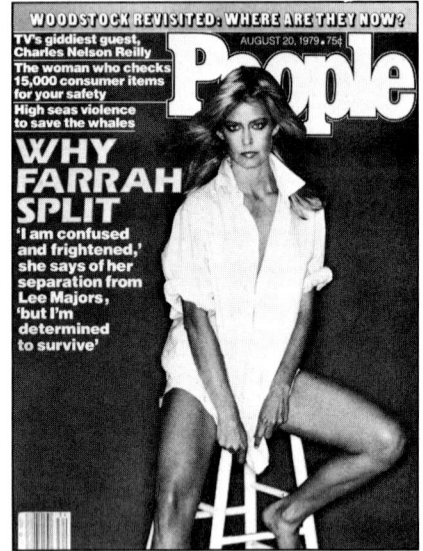

WOODSTOCK REVISITED: WHERE ARE THEY NOW?

TV's giddiest guest, Charles Nelson Reilly

The woman who checks 15,000 consumer items for your safety

High seas violence to save the whales

AUGUST 20, 1979 • 75¢

WHY FARRAH SPLIT

'I am confused and frightened,' she says of her separation from Lee Majors, 'but I'm determined to survive'

1979 BEST-SELLER

The feuding Allman Brothers rock again

FEBRUARY 12, 1979 • 75¢

The tragic toll of fraternity hazing

Sex-change surgery: a tough reporter tells why he became a she

Marcel Marceau: the man behind the mime

MORK'S MINDY

He's the kook in their TV hit, but she's the one who almost cracked in real life

1979 RUNNER-UP (BUT SEE RIGHT)

SYLVIA PORTER ON SURVIVING THE RECESSION

The troubles facing Dr. Kübler-Ross

The manager Farrah dumped after her career foundered

How Gabe Kaplan won $500,000 at poker

OCTOBER 29, 1979 • 75¢

Has MORK blown his cork?

Success shook his life and marriage, but both are solid now

WHOOPS! 1979 WORST ISSUE

John Lennon 1940-1980 A TRIBUTE

DECEMBER 22, 1980 • 95¢

1980 BEST-SELLER

Malpractice: when & how to sue your doctor

Roberta Flack on the rebound

Two psychologists help kids control their TV appetites

What's Saint Laurent peddling now? Opium

OCTOBER 9, 1978 ■ 75¢
14227

People
weekly

JACLYN SMITH

The only bachelor Angel is a nice old-fashioned girl—and trying to do something about it

Top Left Cover

Exclusive: a talk with that ex-CIA agent in Libya
Mary Martin is back
Happy Days' happy hour

NOVEMBER 23, 1981•95¢

People weekly

The Pregnant Princess

Nannies, nappies, names and Lord knows what all: Di and Charles plan for the royal heir

O 10277   47

BOTH MARRIAGE AND PREGNANCY MADE PRINCESS DI A WINNER

Top Right Cover

MARIE OSMOND & a bouquet of celeb brides

JULY 5, 1982•$1.00

People weekly

OH, BOY!

For Diana's 7-pound, 1½-ounce prince, the palace plans a future fit for a king

O 10277   27
724414

DIANA'S GOOD NEWS BECAME 1982'S NO. 2 BEST-SELLER

Bottom Left Cover

AUGUST 16, 1982•$1.15

People weekly

Sinatra, R.J. Wagner, Jill St. John and Carson open an L.A. showplace
Facts of Life in Paris
Broadway's X-rated star

KING OF HEARTS

A royal christening— and a touching moment for Diana and her little prince

O 10277   33
724414

READERS AND SUBJECTS ALIKE CHEERED SWEET WILLIAM

Bottom Right Cover

Love Boat's all-star China cruise

JUNE 27, 1983•$1.25

People weekly

Patricia Neal faces a new ordeal: divorce
Loretta Lynn at a country music fan fair

Happy Birthday
PRINCE WILLIAM

The playmates, playthings and pomp of the royal heir's first year

O 10277   26
724414

THE YOUNG PRINCE RATED A COVER ALL TO HIMSELF IN 1983

October 27, 1975 • 50¢

People weekly

Elton's new hit is Neil Sedaka

The woman behind the Golden Door

ROBERT REDFORD

'Condor' has a plot to save those purple mountain majesties

Sylvia Plath: letters from a tortured life

14227

FEBRUARY 28, 1983 ■ $1.25

People weekly

The Shock of Araby

Brooke Shields

Arabs woo her with jewels but the teen star, on location in Israel, holds out for a prince

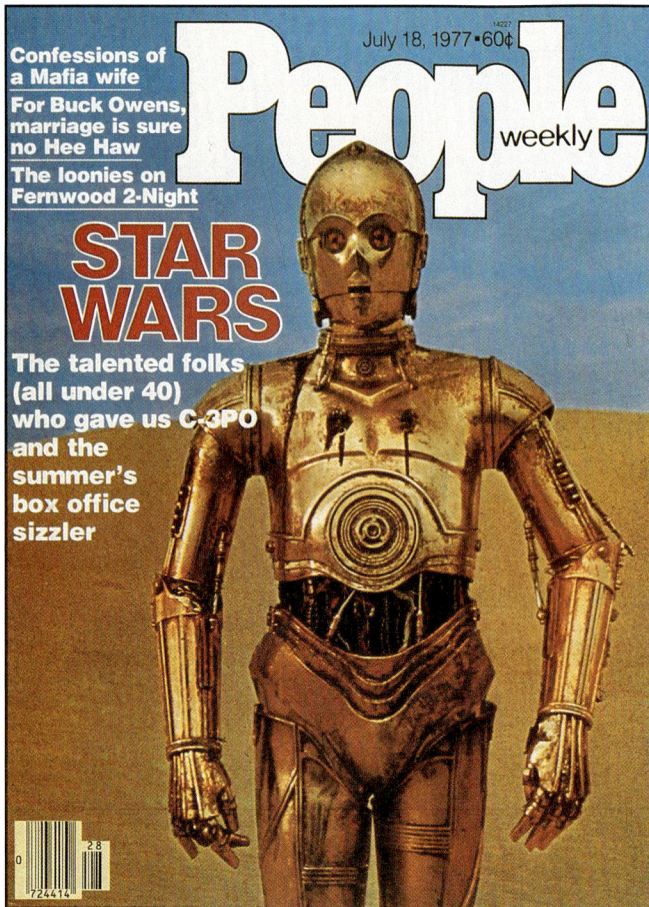

July 18, 1977 • 60¢

People weekly

Confessions of
a Mafia wife

For Buck Owens,
marriage is sure
no Hee Haw

The loonies on
Fernwood 2-Night

STAR WARS

The talented folks
(all under 40)
who gave us C-3PO
and the
summer's
box office
sizzler

SPACE CREATURES LIKE C-3PO SIZZLED AT THE BOX OFFICE

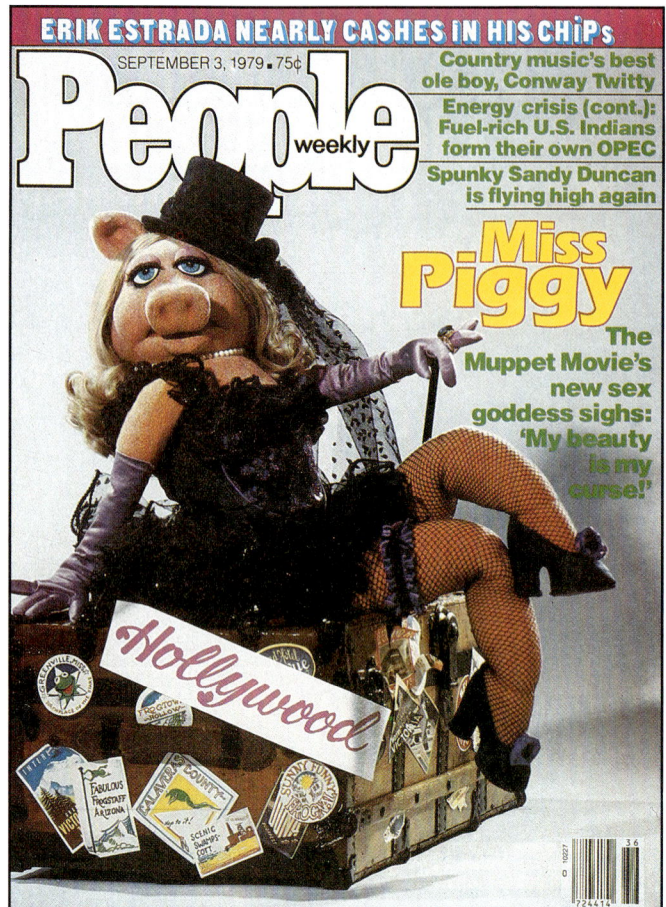

ERIK ESTRADA NEARLY CASHES IN HIS CHiPs

SEPTEMBER 3, 1979 • 75¢

People weekly

Country music's best
ole boy, Conway Twitty

Energy crisis (cont.):
Fuel-rich U.S. Indians
form their own OPEC

Spunky Sandy Duncan
is flying high again

Miss Piggy

The
Muppet Movie's
new sex
goddess sighs:
'My beauty
is my
curse!'

Hollywood

A PUPPET PERHAPS, BUT HER PORKRITUDE WAS PALPABLE

JUNE 28, 1982 $1.00

People weekly

Clint Eastwood rides high
in D.C. and New York

Starch-blocking pills
spark a new diet war

Dallas' elusive Miss Ellie

Wow! A movie to steal America's heart

E.T.

Actor Henry Thomas, 10, and his
extraterrestrial friend

E.T. SO CHARMED VIEWERS HE WAS ON THREE 1982 COVERS

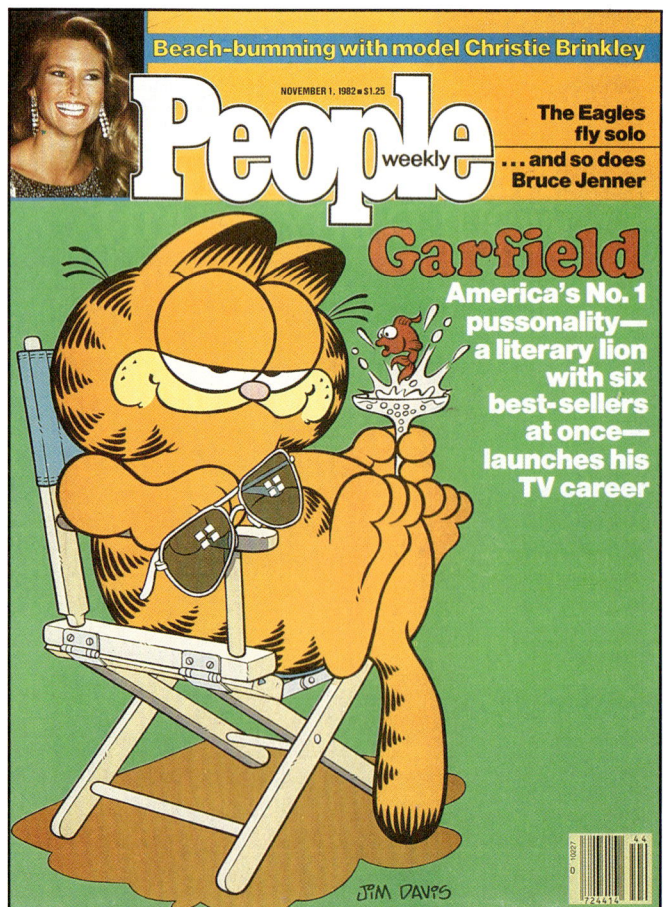

Beach-bumming with model Christie Brinkley

NOVEMBER 1, 1982 $1.25

People weekly

The Eagles
fly solo
...and so does
Bruce Jenner

Garfield

America's No. 1
pussonality—
a literary lion
with six
best-sellers
at once—
launches his
TV career

JIM DAVIS

GARFIELD MADE A FELINE FIRST WITH HIS NOV. 1, 1982 COVER

OCTOBER 22, 1979 ▪ 75¢

THE SEX DRIVE: IS IT STRONGER IN MEN?

Hank Williams Jr. lives up to his C&W legacy

Outtasight! An L.A. orthodontist invents invisible braces

The brave nun who preached to the Pope

People weekly

CHER

She and KISS's GENE SIMMONS bare their life together and marriage thoughts for the first time

March 15, 1976 ▪ 50¢

14227

People

weekly

Rosalynn:
Jimmy Carter's
'secret weapon'

Patty's shrink:
'Anyone can be
brainwashed'

LIZ

Un-Burtoned
again, she
goes home
to mother
—and to Henry

1980 RUNNER-UP

1981 BEST-SELLER

1981 RUNNER-UP

1982 FIRST GATEFOLD

1982 BEST-SELLER

1982 RUNNER-UP

1983 BEST-SELLER

1983 RUNNER-UP

Arts

American originals like Georgia O'Keeffe and Twyla Tharp, and gifted emigrés like Pinchas Zukerman and Zubin Mehta made for an era abundantly rich in art. From painter's canvas to concert halls, PEOPLE readers were witness to creativity in action.

FEAT OF CLAY

In 1975, at age 88, New Mexico painter Georgia O'Keeffe kept a firm grip on life with a male companion 59 years younger and an earthy new medium—pottery.

©DAN BUDNIK 1975 / WOODFIN CAMP

Arts

OFF HIS CHEST

"Drawing is a way of reasoning on paper," said artist/cartoonist Saul Steinberg in 1978. "Essentially what I am playing with is the voyage between perception and understanding."

MICHAEL ABRAMSON/GAMMA-LIAISON

POP'S GRANDPOP

Although he "felt completely out of touch" in the 1970s, modernist Robert Rauschenberg bounced back in '83 with new zip and some handsome made-in-China collages.

IN THE LIGHT

Dismissed by some as "the rich man's Norman Rockwell," Andrew Wyeth and his paintings in 1976 drew the largest crowds ever for a living artist at the Metropolitan Museum.

©ARNOLD NEWMAN

CO RENTMEESTER

DOUBLE THREAT

Crouching, pouncing, glowering and flailing, Marx Brothers fan Zubin Mehta was too showy for some but had the Philharmonics of both New York and Israel well in hand.

©STEVE HANSEN

PRIMA MAESTRA

Conductor Sarah Caldwell founded her own Boston opera company at 33 and in 1976 appeared as the Met's first maestra. "Maybe now that the novelty is wearing off," she said of female firsts, "we'll make more progress."

THE GODFATHER

Called head of the "Kosher Nostra" because of his cultural clout, Isaac Stern got his ears boxed on his 60th birthday by protégés Itzhak Perlman (left) and Pinchas Zukerman.

Arts

©KENN DUNCAN

BOLSHOI STAR

Aleksandr Godunov gave up his wife of eight years in 1979 after he became the first-ever Bolshoi star to defect to the U.S.

©JACK VARTOOGIAN

©MIMI COTTER

HIGH KICKER

A 1970 defector, Natalia Makarova leaped from ballet to Broadway in 1983 to star in the musical comedy *On Your Toes.*

BALLET'S "MR. B"

Ballet is an invitation to "see the music and hear the dance," said New York City Ballet master George Balanchine, who died at 79 in 1983.

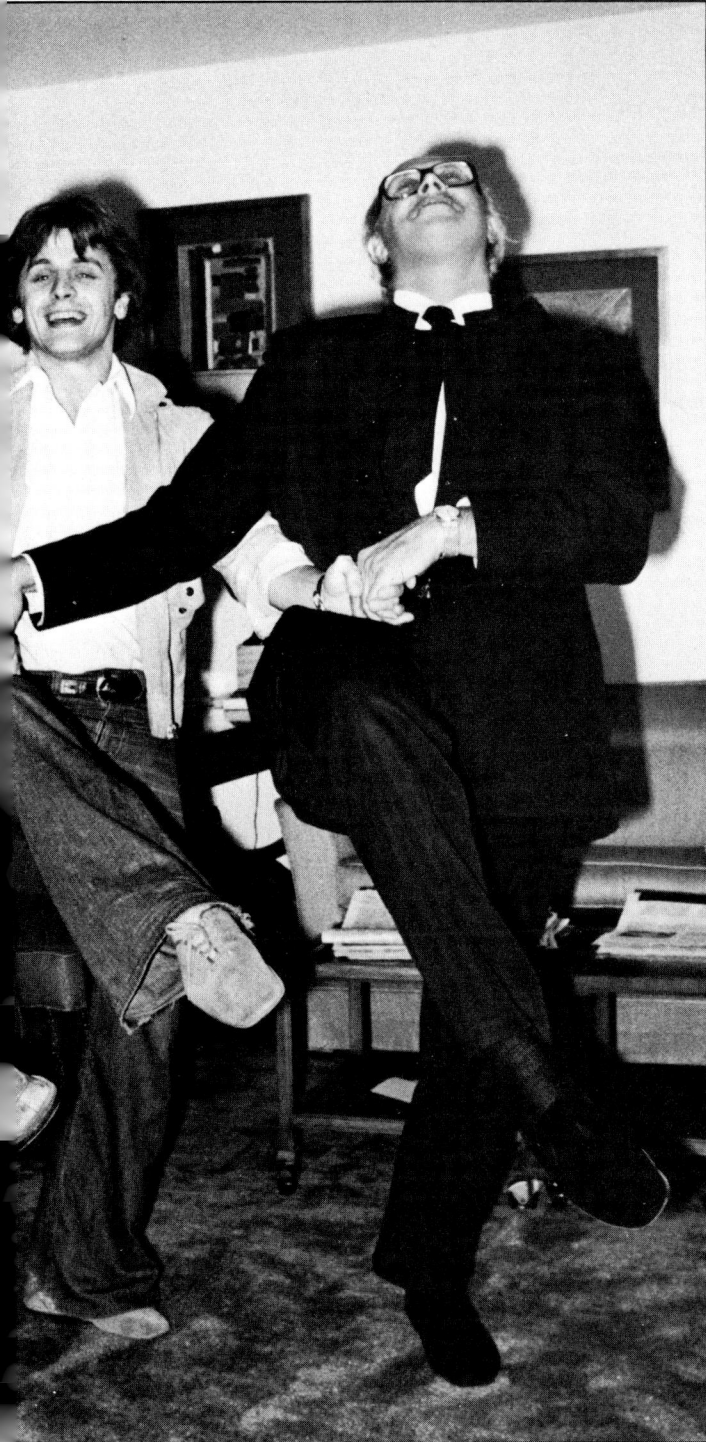

A BORIS LINE

A 1976 memorial concert for Dmitri Shostakovich prompted a jig by the composer's Russian countrymen: poet Joseph Brodsky, dancer Mikhail Baryshnikov and cellist-conductor Mstislav Rostropovich.

STRETCHING OUT

"I came to dance everything," vowed Rudolf Nureyev, who mastered the moderns, including *Moments* by Murray Louis in 1976.

Arts

© JACK VARTOOGIAN

IN THE BAG

Alwin Nikolais reigned as a magus of multimedia with his light shows, electronic music and even body sacks for his dancers.

TAKING A FALL

Overtaxed by work, worry and personal demons, choreographer Alvin Ailey required psychiatric treatment in 1980, then staged a triumphant comeback.

© JACK MITCHELL

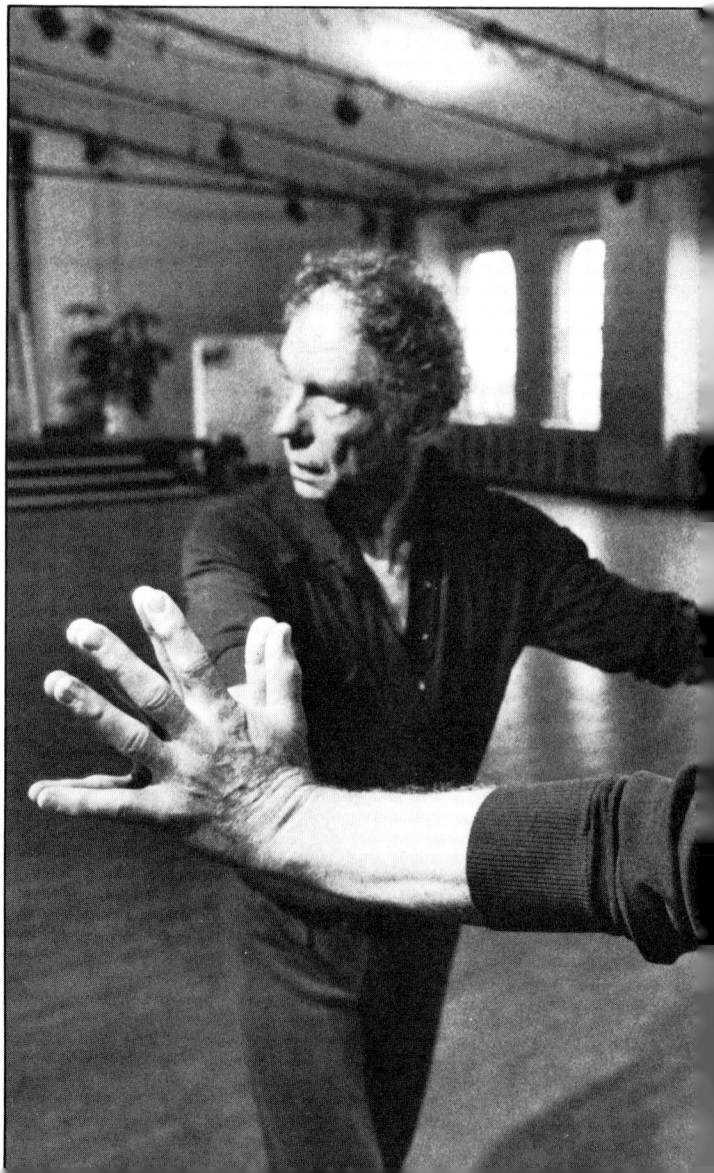

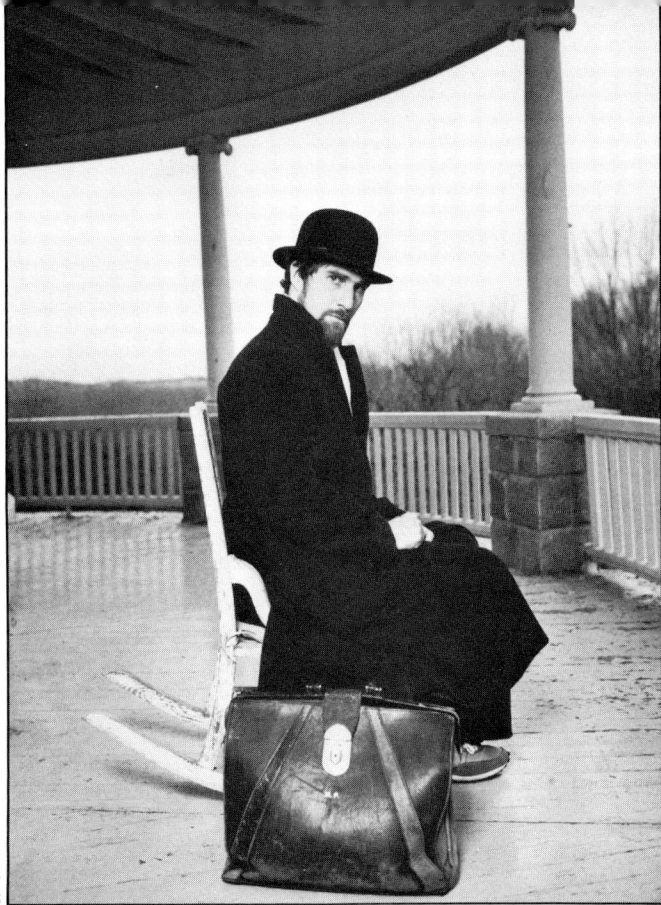

©JACK VARTOOGIAN

COMIC RELIEF

The madcap dances and whimsical tableaux of his company, Pilobolus, made Dartmouth grad Moses Pendleton the Charlie Chaplin of ballet.

HENRY GROSSMAN

©HERBERT MIGDOLL

PRESSING HIS CASE

Maverick modern dance choreographer Merce Cunningham seemed almost traditional after his work played on PBS's *Great Performances* TV series.

TAKING OFF

Indiana-born Twyla Tharp fused blues, rock, ragtime and dance and stepped to the front ranks of avant-garde choreographers.

Arts

Of all the dancing tots Mikhail Baryshnikov uncovered at his American Ballet Theatre, none made as big a splash in 1982 as Susan Jaffe at 20.

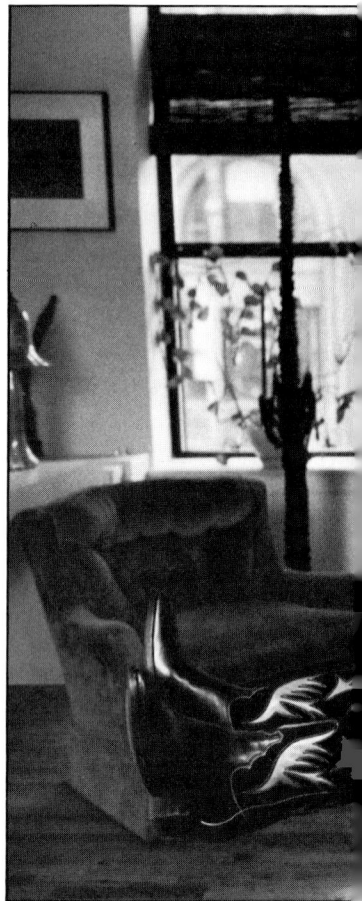

HAVE SLIPPERS, WILL TRAVEL

A pool shark and rock lover, Cynthia Gregory, a/k/a "the Body" in ballet circles, sprang from demure roles in *Swan Lake* to being a fiery Carmen in 1982 and became many male dancers' favorite podner.

©JACK VARTOOGIAN

140

©JACK VARTOOGIAN

©JILL KREMENTZ

©DANIEL S. SORINE

EXIT LAUGHING?

Gelsey Kirkland at 27 hurt so in body (tendinitis), soul (a brief romance with Baryshnikov) and ego (too fragile) that she quit ABT and hoofed it to Europe.

SCOOP!

"Mr. Balanchine, is this a mistake?" bug-eyed Darci Ann Kistler asked, at 16, when first listed as a lead.

141

Arts

WHAT GLORY, PRICE!

"How I've grown!" Leontyne Price warbled after a 1976 Met production of *Aida*. Nights off, the Missisippi carpenter's daughter admitted, "I can't stand the opera."

TENOR CHAMP

Sleeker and more versatile than Pavarotti, Placido Domingo in '82 finally caught up to his rotund rival in popularity in opera's battle of the High C's.

NOTHING LIKE A DAME

Kiri Te Kanawa, a half-European, half-Maori from New Zealand, loved jeans, swigged beer, sang at the Royal Wedding, was dubbed a dame in '82 and warned other sopranos, "Maoris eat their rivals."

LICKIN' GOOD

Not one to accept a cold shoulder, tenor Luciano Pavarotti sampled soprano Renata Scotto's at a 1976 Carnegie Hall recital backstage. Tickled, the diva declared, "Nothing about Luciano surprises me."

HASN'T DRIVEN A FORD LATELY

Reviving a stalled giant with $1.5 billion in loans guaranteed by the Feds, Lee Iacocca got Chrysler speeding along Recovery Road by 1982 and could thumb his nose at Ford, who'd fired him.

It was a discombobulating decade for the high rollers. Like a legend gone wacko, frogs turned into princes and back again, fine knights appeared then vanished in the mists, and fortune's wheel never stopped spinning. 'Twas sort of fabulous.

BEN MARTIN

WINNERS & LOSERS

UNFRIENDLY SKIES

Freddie Laker was ebullient when he got his no-frills, no-reservations New York/London service aloft in 1977, and still chipper when recession, fuel costs and price slashing grounded him in 1982.

145

WINNERS & LOSERS

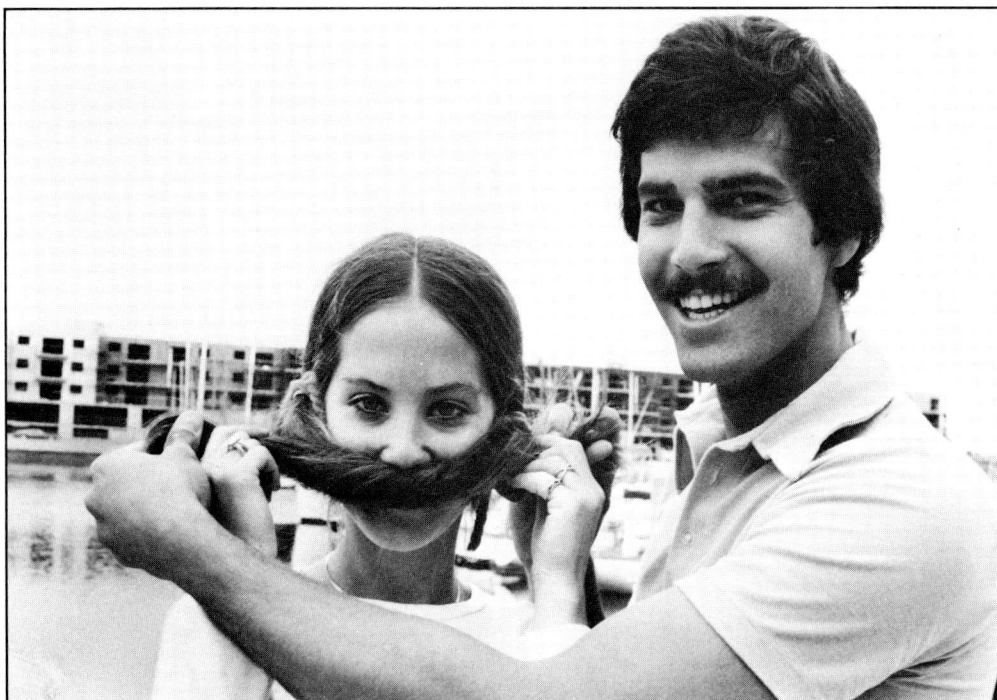

BILL EPPRIDGE

BLOWING HIS COVER

Howard Cosell's yap won him the Most-Boring-Man-on-TV crown in PEOPLE's 1979 reader poll, but, as he showed while umping a celeb paddle tourney in '76, nobody could top him for rug-ged individualism.

SINKING SENSATION

After seven swimming Golds at the 1972 Olympics, Mark Spitz (with wife Suzy) was dubbed "the greatest hero since Lindbergh." Calling early stardom "a terminal illness," he went into real estate.

DAVID HUME KENNERLY/GAMMA-LIAISON

HIGH COURTING

Raised on a ranch, an ex-prexy of the Junior League and former Arizona state senator, family woman Sandra Day O'Connor desegregated the Supreme Court with one oath in 1981.

WINNERS
& LOSERS

AND I'D ALSO
LIKE TO THANK . . .

Oops, racket slipped.
Oops, wrong finger. Never
mind. Jimmy Connors may
have been the baddest boy
when ranked No. 1 in
1975, but in 1983 he was
30, mellower—and no
match for Mac.

GRANTLAND RICE POEM, REVISED FOR J. McENROE

For when the One Great Scorer/Comes to mark against your name,/Pray He writes how oft you won or lost,/Not how you played the game.

WINNERS & LOSERS

LOVE IN BLOOM

Your basic virgin meets a nobleman; they marry chaste. The plot served Barbara Cartland 307 times by 1981, making her "grateful I can give of myself." Sigh.

OH, BROTHER!

Just a kid with old knees, Joe Namath wobbled off the gridiron after 13 gutsy seasons to star in films like 1978's *Avalanche Express* (where he clowned in monk's robes) and TV ads. But win or lose, the world still gave its regards to Broadway Joe.

HENRY GROSSMAN

A shark captured in oils by a friend—and the one painted in prose by himself—gave Benchley plenty of reason to smile.

PETER BENCHLEY

The Heir of a Literary Family Surfaces With His Own Best-seller

BY JOAN OLIVER

Slender, tall and movie-star handsome, with eyes like the deep blue sea, Peter Benchley did not inherit the resemblance to a benevolent sea lion which distinguished his famous grandfather—humorist Robert Benchley—and which, slightly refined, was bestowed on Peter's father, writer Nathaniel Benchley. Instead, Peter is the fortunate legatee of the writing dynasty's quirky wit and knack for spinning a devilishly good tale.

In February (1974) the 33-year-old Benchley published *Jaws,* his first novel. Within eight weeks, it leaped to No. 2 position on the *New York Times'* best-seller list. Before the book was even off the presses, it had already earned over $1 million, including $575,000 for U.S. paperback rights alone, and from sales to book clubs, foreign publishers and the film's producers. The movie version, which Benchley wrote, is already in production for Universal.

The tale of a great white shark grew out of young Benchley's fascination with the killer fish triggered by family fishing expeditions off Nantucket. As he became a successful journalist-reporter on the *Washington Post,* free-lancer for such magazines as LIFE and *The New Yorker,* and an editor of *Newsweek*—his shark-watching continued. In the 1960s he capitalized on his interest with two magazine articles, not long after a 4,500-pound great white shark was taken off Long Island's Montauk Point. A few years later he was assigned to do a piece about Southampton—Long Island's tony watering place. Benchley remembers thinking, "My God, if that kind of thing can happen around the beaches of Long Island, and I know Southampton, why not put the two together."

The star attraction of Benchley's book is the marauding monster whose savage attacks Benchley describes with horrifying clarity. Of a child snatched from a raft, he writes: "Nearly half the fish had come clear of the water, and it slid forward and down in a belly-flopping motion, grinding the mass of flesh and bone and rubber. The boy's legs were severed at the hips, and they sank, spinning slowly, to the bottom."

Like his father and grandfather, Benchley was educated at Exeter and Harvard. His life today is centered in a small yellow frame house in Pennington, N.J., which he occupies, amid genteely shabby furniture, with his wife, Wendy, and children, Tracy and Clayton. He does find his sudden fame "awesome," but he's glad about "not having to hustle magazine pieces anymore." Still, he doesn't expect the family's lifestyle will change much. "Oh, we'll probably move closer to Princeton. We play tennis and take the kids to school there."

April 15, 1974

Following the 1975 movie, Jaws, *Benchley wrote* The Deep *and* The Island, *which were also made into films. His most recent book is* The Girl of the Sea of Cortez.

MARGAUX HEMINGWAY

A Famous Beauty Becomes One For Whom Bells Toll

BY JOHN NEARY

This Hemingway was not like the other Hemingway, the old one. She was a different Hemingway. She was his granddaughter. She was very good. There were things that she would not talk about, her ex-husband for one. She wanted to forget him, she said. "All experience is good," she said. "But you have to move on to better things." She giggled and looked at the one she was with now. It was a warm look. "Love for me," she said, "is truth."

They were in Venice, this Hemingway, the one they call Margaux, and the one she was with, whose name is Bernard Foucher. She is 23; Bernard, a Venezuelan, is 39, and is, Margaux said, "my best friend and lover." And Venice is a good place to be with someone like that—just as Ernest, the old Hemingway, said it was.

On television Margaux rides the inner tube for Fabergé commercials. It is what one must do for $1 million. But not in Venice. There she was, as the grandfather wrote of the fantasy women he loved in his novel, *Across the River and Into the Trees:* "Shining in her youth and tall striding beauty, and the carelessness the wind had made of her hair. She had pale, almost olive colored skin, a profile that could break your, or any one else's heart . . ."

Nobody mentioned the old one, the grandfather, but the couple did as he wrote: "They got down into the gondola and there was the same magic, as always, of the light hull and the sudden displacement that you made." And that was the way it was, for Margaux and Bernard in the gondola. She and Bernard, her lover, were in Italy to play

tennis to help the Venice in Peril Fund. There, too, were Sonny Bono and Susie Coelho, Valerie Perrine and Charlton (whom his friends call "Chuck") Heston. But Margaux had a pulled tendon. As Jake Barnes might have said, "It was a rotten way to be wounded."

And so it happened, just as the old one had written, after she and Bernard "had paid the *gondoliere,* who was unknowing, yet knowing all . . . they walked into the Piazzetta and then across the great, cold wind-swept square that was hard and old under their feet. They walked holding close and hard in their sorrow and their happiness."

September 11, 1978

Margaux married Bernard Foucher in January 1980. No longer employed by Fabergé, she is a sometime movie actress.

Just as Renata and the Colonel did in Grandpapa's *Across the River and Into the Trees,* **Margaux Hemingway and Bernard Foucher snuggled together in a Venetian gondola.**

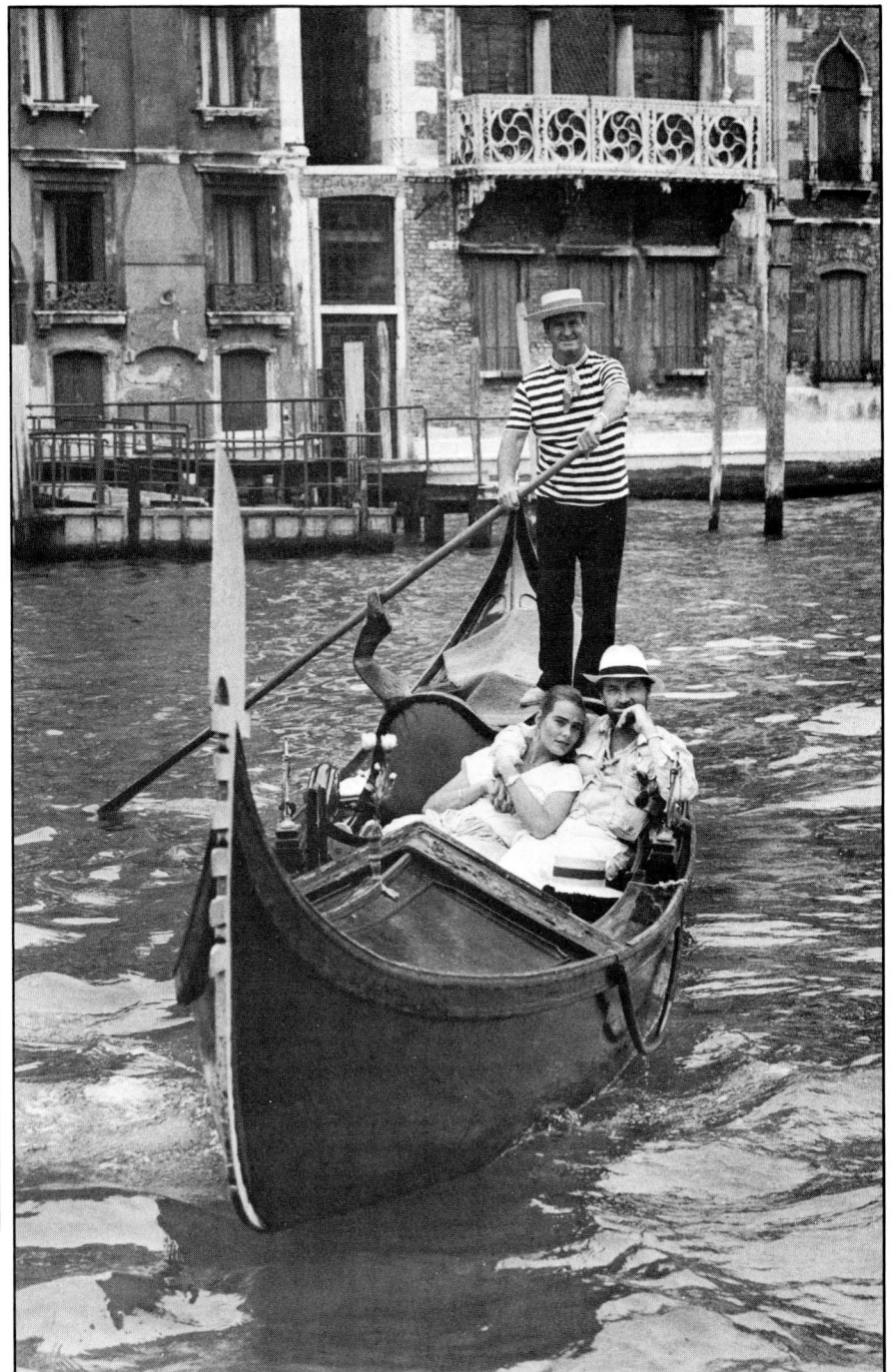

MISS PIGGY

A Perky Porker Hits Hollywood and Leaves 'Em Squealing

BY BRAD DARRACH

A sunburst blonde lolls on lavender satin sheets. Her mouth is large, scarlet, half-open. Her blank blue eyes smolder like sapphires in candlelight. "My beauty," she murmurs breathily as her sensuous snout writhes with allure, "is my curse!" Swooning toward her, the camera reveals the luscious pink of her skin, the ripe contours (27-20-32) of her pigure. But to adoring millions it matters not that the lady is a hog. They worship Miss Piggy as the acme of porkritude, a pig of perfection, a new international sex goddess whose image has been stamped on pop culture in indelible oink.

Miss Piggy burst into celebrity as the star of *The Muppet Show,* a huge TV hit that is aired in 106 countries and seen every week by 260 million viewers—among them Sophia Loren and the Prime Minister of Britain. In 1979, after only 11 weeks in release, Miss Piggy's first feature film, *The Muppet Movie,* had grossed $50 million, and the Cincinnati-based CAMPO (Committee to Award Miss

Critics saw hints of a fiery Anne Bancroft and soulful Greta Garbo in Miss Piggy's film debut, but the porcine star struck a positively Garland-esque pose for her 1979 PEOPLE cover.

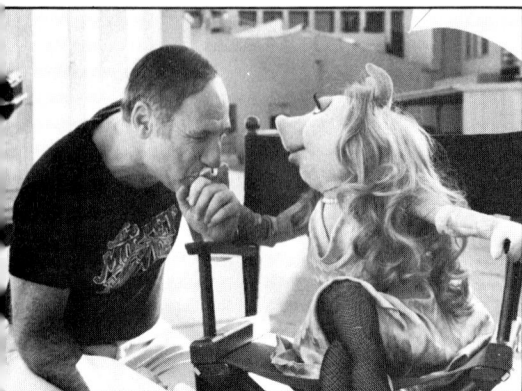

Mel Brooks, who played a mad scientist in Miss Piggy's film, said, "She's non-kosher, but I fell head over heels in love."

Piggy the Oscar) has amassed 20,000 fan letters demanding that she be named Best Actress of the Year.

She wowed critics. Exulted one: "Miss Piggy combines the explosiveness of Anne Bancroft, the vulnerability of Judy Garland and the soul of Greta Garbo in a body that drives men mad. She is contradictory, mysterious, baffling. She is Woman."

Contradictory indeed—but always the actress. One instant she is playing the Arrogant Superstar, snarling at her beefy litter bearers as she finishes her big Cleopatra scene: "Awright, meat! Let's move it!" The next she is Daddy's Little Darling, giggling and cooing: "I'll only be an eeeeentsy-teentsy minute! Kissy, kissy!" Then without warning she drops a karate chop on a luckless reporter who has inquired about her weight problem. "When she looks in the mirror," says the star's dress designer, Calista Hendrickson, "Miss Piggy sees Twiggy—and you better not forget it."

Moments later, pignacity phases into

Blanche AvoirduBois as Miss Piggy enacts her idea of what it's like to be a lady: Simpering and smirking, she parades her culture ("Are you speaking to *moi*?"), yet dresses up as Brünnhilde to sing—Puccini? When her agent calls, Miss Piggy transforms on the spot into a Capitalist Pig: "Okay, Marty, whaddya got? A commercial? How much? [Grunt.] *Take it!*" Yet she wilts like a broiled violet when the director cuts her solo. Then a glimpse of Rudolf Nureyev on the set brings out the beast in her. She pursues him into a steam bath; when he staggers out his towel is at half-mast.

"Miss Piggy seems complex," says Frank Oz, the enigmatic Svengali figure who has guided her career and acts as her spokesman, "because she is a seething mass of conflicts. She's very vulnerable, and she's been hurt a lot. It's hard enough being a woman in our society. It's even harder being a pig. On top of that," he acknowledged to PEOPLE correspondent Fred Hauptfuhrer, "Miss Piggy doesn't have the greatest body or the greatest voice. So there's been rejection and pain. To protect her feelings, she's built up layers of defenses. But underneath the glamour and the bravado she's very serious and very courageous."

Miss Piggy's psychiatrist probes a little deeper. "She's now at the point," he confides indiscreetly, "where she could afford to ease up on her career and start a personal life. She wants to, but she's afraid to. As a star she gets adoration without risk. She also enjoys wealth and power. She's had her consciousness raised," he concludes, "but she still likes diamonds."

There were no diamonds and not much consciousness in the Midwestern barnyard where Miss Piggy was born—only Miss Piggy knows when, and she isn't telling. According to Oz, Miss Piggy's father chased after other sows and her mother had so many piglets she never found time to develop her mind. "I'll die before I live like that!" Miss Piggy screamed and ran away.

Desperate, she took a stage name, Laverne, and started in the back line of the Muppet Show's chorus in 1976. But she didn't stay there long. She had fallen head over trotters for Kermit, the frog who emcees the show, and during the performance, overwhelmed by desire for that puny pea-green body, she crushed the frog in a hog hug. Struck by her screen presence and the drama in the situation, Oz persuaded Muppet producer Jim Henson to co-star Miss Piggy and the reluctant Rhett of her Scarlett daydreams. The rest is hogstory.

Miss Piggy's passion for her "virile frog" rules her life. Easygoing, matter-of-fact, self-sufficient, Kermit is the calm green eye in the hurricane of Miss Piggy's emotions. "There are two openings in life for a frog," he says philosophically. "He can go into show business—or he can wind up on a plate. It isn't easy being green."

It's Miss Piggy's favorite color, and his indifference drives her wild. She hates exercise, but to get in better shape she has taken up pig-pong. She bats her enormous eyelashes till she blows the frog down and keeps asking him lewdly when he wants to open his birthday present. "Piggy mummy, Kermie daddy," she twitters, imagining hogly matrimony. "Wouldn't hims like a little pog?" Kermit shudders. All he can see is an endless succession of "bouncing baby figs." But Miss Piggy refuses to admit rejection. "He wants me desperately," she says with a self-satisfied sigh. "This little green thing crawling toward me, begging me to marry him. It's a sad sight."

Recently, to make Kermit jealous, Miss Piggy has launched some flamboyant affairs. "The Queen tried to fix me up with Prince Charles," she told the British press. "The Royal Family wants nothing but the best for their boy." But La Pig had other fish to fry. "I don't want to name names," she says, "because there are many big stars involved." But Elliott Gould fessed up. "I turned down Miss Universe," he says, "but I couldn't turn down Miss Piggy." And her co-star in The Muppet Movie, Charles Durning, asks with a sigh: "How can you say no to a lady with 16 breasts?"

But by far the most insidious buzz-buzz is that Miss Piggy may not actually be a pig at all! Attributed to a disaffected pigolo who had been living high on the hog, the rumor has it that Miss Piggy is a puppet. In fact, according to this disturbing report, there have been 11 separate puppets. Made of soft foam rubber, allegedly of the same kind used in air-conditioning filters, the Miss Piggy puppets are said to wear out in six months. Early versions of the glamorous hambone were sculpted out of foam-rubber blocks; more recent versions have been formed of liquid latex poured into a mold. Her eyes are felt and plastic, and on each eye she wears two sets of false lashes.

Most of the 11 Miss Piggys, says the whispering campaign, haven't even had gams. Instead, the story goes, a sleeve runs from the bottom of the skirt to the neck of the hollow skull—and the sleeve is tailored to fit the arm of the ubiquitous Mr. Oz. Proponents of the puppet theory believe that Oz speaks Miss Piggy's lines and manipulates her lush body.

Oz (short for Oznowicz) is, in fact, producer Henson's most brilliant puppeteer. Now 35, he grew up in Oakland, Calif. and got interested in puppets because they were his parents' hobby. He admits he animates The Muppet Show's Fozzie and Animal and Sesame Street's Cookie Monster and Bert. But he denies flatly that he's Miss Piggy's puppet master. "I just give her a hand," he says. Miss Piggy emphatically agrees.

Miss Piggy is mildly irritated by all these inswineuations—she sees them as attempts to strip her of her pignity. But she is truly outraged by reports that producer Henson, worried because she is stealing The Muppet Show from the other characters, may try to reduce her roles. "If Henson cuts his star," she squeals, "he cuts his own throat. Without me, who will tune in just to watch a lot of stupid puppets?" Then has success spoiled history's most successful pig? "That's a lot of swill," snorts Miss Piggy. "I am still just little moi, the same gorgeous and supremely talented pig."

September 3, 1979
Time has not sty-mied Miss Piggy's career. Since this story appeared she has written a book, cut an aerobic dance exercise album and appeared in a second Muppet movie.

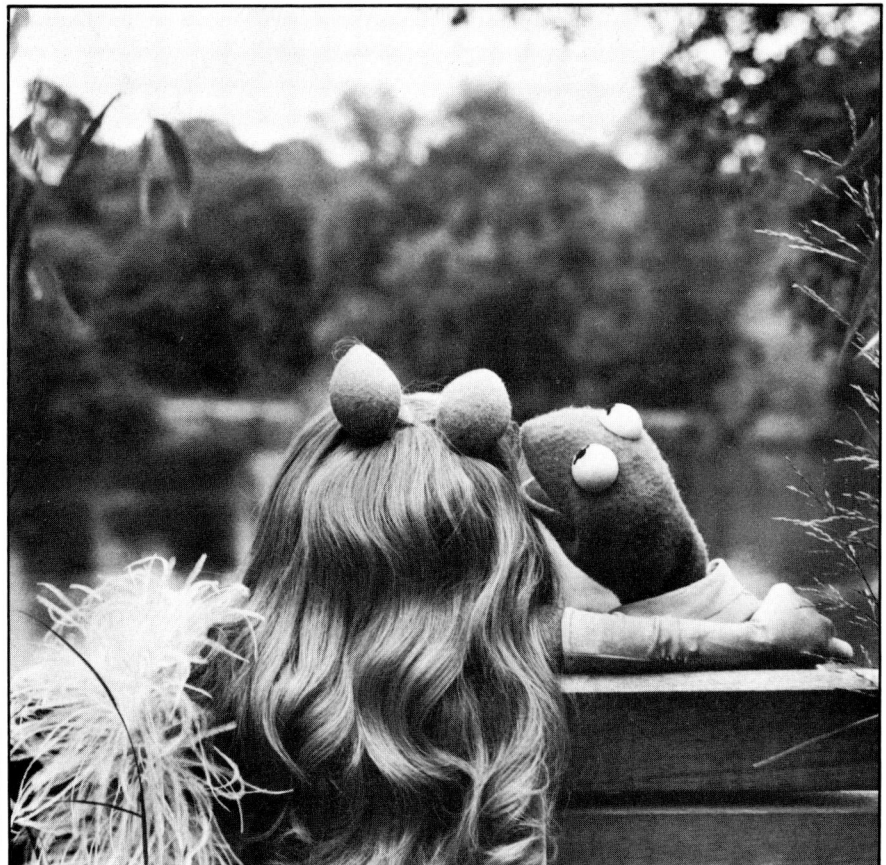

Although Kermit's feelings for Miss Piggy have always seemed somewhat mixed, the determinedly liberated lady described their relationship as "desperately close."

JOSEPH HELLER

An Obscure Disease Holds a Noted Writer in its Grip

BY JOSEPH HELLER

In December 1981, Heller, author of the best-sellers Catch-22, Something Happened *and* Good as Gold, *suddenly fell victim to Guillain-Barré syndrome, a rare form of paralysis that strikes the central nervous system. Although 80 percent of its victims eventually regain their health, full recovery from the viral ailment can take months and sometimes even years. Since describing his ordeal to* PEOPLE *senior writer Cheryl McCall, Heller, now 61, continued to make steady improvement. He and wife Shirley, who were married in 1945, went to divorce court in 1983, and work proceeded on a draft of his fourth novel.*

Not surprisingly, I'd never heard of this disease before. I first recognized something was unusual on a Saturday morning when I was having trouble swallowing and I couldn't take my sweater off over my head. That same day I went to the gym. I was unable to bring my head to my knees in the warm-up exercises, and I couldn't run my usual four miles. I jogged about a mile and a half. I went out that evening for dinner with a couple of friends and I had trouble swallowing the vegetables, but I didn't think much of that either. When I woke up the next day, my arms felt weak and I felt tired. I called the doctor at home and gave him my symptoms, and he diagnosed it as Guillain-Barré syndrome right away—just because it came on that suddenly. That afternoon, my right knee buckled as I was entering Mt. Sinai Hospital. A few minutes later, I was in intensive care. It hits that quickly. The neurologist did a very valuable thing: He said, "You're probably going to have a mild case"—which turned out not to be true—but he said, "You'll recover fully. You'll get it all back." I didn't ask what I was losing.

The first night I was there, the man next to me died, and every few days somebody would die. There were four beds, and for most of my three weeks in there, I was the only one not in a coma. After three or four days, I was scared stiff without realizing it. I was afraid to go to sleep, but I was dying for sleep. My eyes kept falling shut, but I kept snapping my head up. I felt if I fell off to sleep, I would never wake up, I would never take another breath. By the fifth day, I thought I was going out of my mind. A neurologist suggested a psychiatrist, and one saw me every day until I left Mt. Sinai.

He told me that I was not psychotic, but that there is something called "intensive care psychosis." My reactions were normal. If I had had any different reaction to being there, then there was reason to worry. Consciously, I was not afraid of dying or permanent paralysis. Unconsciously, I suppose I was scared stiff. I don't think I ever slept more than two hours at a time—even when I got a private room.

I was never totally paralyzed. The word they use is "quadraparetic." The disease progressed quickly. I could not move at all after eight to 10 days. They told me I'd be weak, but I didn't know what weak meant.

At Heller's East Hampton pool, therapist Don Shaw put the author through sometimes excruciating exercises to rebuild atrophied muscles.

The only thing left intact by this disease was my sense of humor—and my feet. For more than three months, I couldn't raise my head. I couldn't swallow, so I had a suction tube in my throat for the secretions. I was fed through a tube in my nose for more than four months. I couldn't read after the third day because I couldn't hold a book or turn the pages. I lost between 20 and 30 pounds.

Slowly, as the movement in my arms and fingers began to return, the disease was advancing in other areas. The right side of my face and tongue were being affected. After a while, I didn't have enough energy to keep my right eye closed. There was a kind of loss of pride about some things, but that didn't last long—I'd ask the nurse to do things for me. I could not reach my groin with my hands to urinate, for instance. I stopped biting my nails—which I've done since first grade—because I couldn't get my fingers to my mouth. And if I could have, I didn't have the strength in my jaw to bite them. Having nails is a sort of serendipitous side benefit to Guillain-Barré.

I learned to love the nurses and therapists, and I learned more from them than the doctors because they read up on the disease and explained it to me. Future Presidents would be wise to turn to the medical profession rather than Wall Street for their Secretaries of the Treasury. Doctors do have an eye on money. After my insurance had expired, I had to borrow $60,000 for medical expenses. Unless you have workman's compensation or are indigent, this disease can wipe you out. It's very expensive to get sick; it's a luxury to recuperate.

If this disease hit anybody a second time, the person would give up. I would. I wouldn't want to go through it again. You don't fight Guillain-Barré, you surrender to it. For the five months I couldn't move, my friends took care of my personal affairs for me. Speed Vogel moved into my apartment and assumed my identity. He's a very competent artist, and he learned to duplicate my signature, write checks for me and autograph books. He wore new clothes I had bought and broke them in for me. He also visited me every day. Another friend, Julius Green, who had different talents, figured out my insurance policies. And my children, Erica, 30, and Teddy, 26, would do things for me or bring me things. My wife and I had already been separated for a year when I got sick so I discouraged her from visiting.

One of my friends who did come was Mel Brooks, to my amazement. He was drawn there just by the sheer horror of this disease. He said he knew all about Guillain-Barré because he had a book on it. I laughed scornfully. Lots of people have books but no one commits them to memory like Mel does. When Dustin Hoffman

In an antique wooden wheelchair, a gift from old friend Speed Vogel, a recovering Heller resumed work on his novel-in-progress.

showed up, the nurses got a big kick out of it. He brought me a Sony Walkman and cassettes and brushed my teeth for me. He called his doctor and came back with a list of the symptoms for Guillain-Barré—he was worried he was going to get it too. Mario Puzo felt ill just walking into intensive care and wanted to leave immediately.

If anything, this whole ordeal has deepened my friendship with a lot of people because of the solicitude that they've showed—and the love. Just as I avoided thinking I'd ever be seriously ill, I shied away from the word love, and the concept of love, as it existed between me and these people. I realize now that love does exist between me and a large number of people, and I'm very glad. It doesn't embarrass me. It took something like this to bring us together. I'll be grateful to Speed, Julius, my nurse, Valerie Humphries, and other friends for the rest of my life.

When I came out of the Rusk Rehabilitation Institute on May 14 after four months, I knew I would have to go back to living alone because I was estranged from my wife, and my children have small apartments of their own. Speed and Valerie were indispensable because I still couldn't stand up and had to use a wheelchair. There's a line in *Something Happened* that I stole from Speed. "A friend in need is no friend of mine." It's lucky he's forgotten that. While Speed took a much-needed vacation in

Cannes and Valerie returned to day nursing, my brother, Lee, came up from Florida to New York to stay with me for a month.

Then Speed, Valerie and I came out here to my house in East Hampton so I can recuperate. They drive, cook, shop and pick things up for me. I can dress and shower myself now and get in and out of bed. My therapist, Don Shaw, comes three times a week, and the progress is encouraging.

I'm feeling very productive because I'm working in two areas, recuperating and writing a book. I exercise every day in the pool. Getting better requires a lot of concentration on my part, and everything I do, from walking 50 yards to the mailbox to unloading the dishwasher, is therapy. I've been able to write because a friend arranged for me to use a word processor in place of a typewriter, which is hard for me to handle. Getting the paper in and rolling it up to make corrections requires more strength than I have in my arms and fingers. So I write longhand, rewrite on the word processor, and then give it to Valerie to type because she was a secretary before she was a nurse.

My novel is about one-fourth done, over 330 pages of a first draft now. I was not thinking of the book at all while I was in the hospital, but already I'm using the whole experience. Certain thoughts and sensations can be used almost humorously. I hope to have the first draft done by next summer. I thought I'd be able to continue writing much sooner and more rapidly—but I always felt that way even when I was healthy.

One thing this illness did was to answer a lot of questions for me. I had been very unsettled and confused since the dissolution of my marriage. I had no idea where I wanted to go or what I wanted to do. I was a stranger to myself with lots of choices. Guillain-Barré pinned me down, removed the choices and gave a strong organization to my life. I also have *real* problems now. I owe $60,000, and I may have to borrow another $25,000 before I can start making money again. But look at all the money I saved on expensive lunches and dinners when I was hospitalized.

Sometimes I get pessimistic and feel that I might never be able to run again. I long to do that. I long to be able to walk out of the house alone or go down the stairs. I get real feelings of disappointment whenever I realize I might not be doing as well as I think. I'd like to get back to a normal life—which for me involved going a lot of places.

Still, I've been lucky most of my life. When I was a bombardier in World War II, I thought it was *safe*. I flew 60 missions, and I think we only lost two planes in my squad. It was luck because shortly before I went overseas, the casualties were very high. I was lucky there. I may be lucky with this illness.

August 23, 1982

LAURENCE OLIVIER

The Role of First Actor Suits This Noble Lord

BY CHRISTOPHER P. ANDERSEN

With its cool marble walls and burnished yew paneling, the Grill Room of London's legendary Savoy Hotel has not changed much since that evening in 1935—except that back then men were required to wear white tie to supper. "She was sitting right there," says the elderly gentleman, putting down his martini glass and pointing to a vacant table nestled against a pillar, not 10 feet away. "Except for seeing her on the stage, it was the first time I ever set eyes on that exquisite face. Yes, she saw me, too. But she was with a young man who looked very much in love, and I supposed that they were, to put it vulgarly, 'at it.' "

Before leaving the Grill that night, however, Laurence Olivier and his first wife, Jill Esmond, introduced themselves to Vivien Leigh and invited her and her first husband for a weekend at the Oliviers' country house. "It was," smiles Olivier, still gazing at the vacant table through the mist of nearly a half-century, "like any first act of the period, don't you think?"

Before there were Taylor and Burton, or even Tracy and Hepburn, there were Olivier and Leigh. The scandalous extramarital affair that ensued after their encounter at the Savoy made front-page headlines on both sides of the Atlantic, and by the time the brooding Heathcliff of *Wuthering Heights* and *Gone With the Wind*'s Scarlett O'Hara divorced their respective spouses to wed one another in 1940, they had become the First Couple of stage and screen.

Their reign would not be a happy one. Olivier, 75, recalls Leigh's formidable sexual demands (aggravated, he admits, by his own recurring problem with premature ejaculation), her infidelities (with actor Peter Finch, among others) and her descent into mental illness. Once, while on vacation in 1953, Olivier dispatched longtime friends Stewart Granger and David Niven to check up on his manic-depressive wife. They discovered Vivien balancing precariously on an upstairs banister, nude.

Olivier denies that his 1982 memoirs were perhaps *too* explicit: "There have been a thousand biographies of Henry VIII, but he never wrote about himself. Imagine how wonderful it would be to pick up Henry VIII's diary and read, 'Met this charming little tart last night, named Anne something.' "

Olivier's pretense-pricking wit and easy charm belie bouts in the last 15 years with a litany of ailments: prostate cancer, appendicitis, an obstructed kidney, thrombosis, pneumonia and, since 1974, dermatopolymyositis, a muscle-wasting disease that Olivier sees as his most formidable opponent. These afflictions have taken their toll: Olivier moves cautiously now, deliberately. But the voice, the flamboyant gestures and exuberance are, well, pure Olivier.

For health reasons, His Lordship has declared himself to be on the wagon, but during lunch at the Savoy he downs his martini, four glasses of wine—three red, one white—and two brandies. "I'm doing this just for you," he winks. "I want to sparkle. And I thought it might be a nice touch if, toward the end, I just slithered to the floor."

For all the controversy, the saga of Laurence Olivier and Vivien Leigh (she died at 54 in 1967 from tuberculosis) pales in comparison to his extraordinary achievements. From his rapturous Romeo to his overpowering Othello, Olivier has earned a place as the most famous Shakespearean performer ever, the ideal against which classical actors are measured. Meanwhile, for his film *Henry V,* he received a special Academy Award in 1946 as actor/producer/director, and two years later was named Best Actor for *Hamlet*. (He also earned an honorary Oscar for his "lifetime of contribution to the art of film" in 1979.)

Millions more know him not only from *Wuthering Heights* but also as the star of such movies as *Rebecca, Pride and Prejudice, The Entertainer* and, more recently, *Marathon Man* and *The Boys From Brazil.* Olivier was knighted in 1947 and eventually became the first actor in English history ever to be elevated to the House of Lords.

Although he recalls putting on little plays for his mother's amusement (she died when he was 12), that he should ever have become an actor genuinely amazes Olivier. The youngest of a London parson's three children, he is still haunted by his impoverished early years. Like Marilyn Monroe, who would be his co-star and temperamental nemesis during the filming of 1957's *The Prince and the Showgirl,* Olivier was allowed to bathe only after other members of

Sir Laurence Olivier showed just a few of his

the family had first used the water in the tub. "You get to that point," he says, "where you've either got to give up or get the hell out. Anybody who has ever suffered poverty like that knows *exactly* what I mean."

After attending St. Edwards School in Oxford on a scholarship and an apprenticeship with the Birmingham Repertory Theatre, Olivier at 23 appeared in his first hit with Noël Coward and Gertrude Lawrence on stage in 1930's *Private Lives.* Three years later, Olivier was called to Hollywood and then fired from *Queen Christina* by the film's star, Greta Garbo. "She was an absolute magician in her medium and had every right to get rid of me," he says. "Of course, she's dead now, isn't she? *No?* Well, in that case, if you ever meet her, tell her I'd *love* to treat her to lunch—if she could bear it."

Following the swashbuckling style set by John Barrymore, Olivier soon came to be

facets. "What is acting but lying, and what is good acting but convincing lying?"

regarded in London as the most physical of all Shakespearean actors. In *Macbeth,* for example, he broke a sword with such force it flew into the audience; in *Hamlet,* he leapt from a 14-foot-high platform, landing on an actor and knocking him cold.

From the beginning, Olivier has worked "from the outside in," plastering on false noses and makeup and burrowing under the skin of his character. "Larry hates to be his actual self," observed Michael Caine, Olivier's co-star in 1972's *Sleuth.* Olivier winces at the notion. "Too damn psychiatric," he says. "I really don't know what I'm like, and I'm not sure that I want to."

In fact, Olivier's conversation is laced with self-remorse. "The worst part of me—the most boring part—is my guilt complex. I feel almost responsible for the fall of Adam and Eve." He still blames himself for "some-

how causing" Leigh's mental problems. "Once you have those feelings, they don't go away. It was all my fault, of course. Everything is. What isn't? Now that I've admitted it, I'm looking for a little absolution."

These days, Olivier and his third wife, actress Joan Plowright, divide their time between a town house in London's Chelsea district and a country house ("*Please* call it a cottage") in West Sussex. Olivier's white Bentley makes the trip in 90 minutes. In the country, he rises at 5:30 a.m. and spends "a good hour alone, thinking" before doing 40 laps in his 40-foot indoor pool.

Clearly, the focus of Olivier's life is his brood of youngsters by Plowright. Two of their three children plan to follow their parents into show business. "No, I don't worry that they'll be compared to me," their father shrugs. "I won't be around to be compared to. I've timed the whole thing perfectly."

One reason Olivier gives for working so hard—10 films between 1977 and 1983 alone—is to leave his family "well-provided for." After tackling *King Lear* for British television, he wants to try the part of Willy Loman in Arthur Miller's *Death of a Salesman.* He bristles at the suggestion that he stoops to doing second-rate material. "My excuse has been that I'm doing it for the money, but it's not true. For me, working is the only thing. If I stop, I'll drop."

Actress-author Lilli Palmer, a longtime chum of Olivier's, recently felt she finally "had to tell him what a great figure he is. While Larry sat in total silence, I went on and on, comparing him to other artistic geniuses of our time like Picasso and Stravinsky. When I finally finished, Larry looked at me and said, 'Well, don't stop. I'm rather enjoying this.'" So, Lord Olivier, are we.

January 10, 1983

STAGE

HENRY GROSSMAN

From *A Chorus Line* and *The Wiz* to *Dreamgirls*, *Cats* and *Nine*, Broadway audiences rated high kickers over high drama, Fosse and Bennett over Albee and Beckett—and reinvigorated oldies like *On Your Toes* were only a step behind.

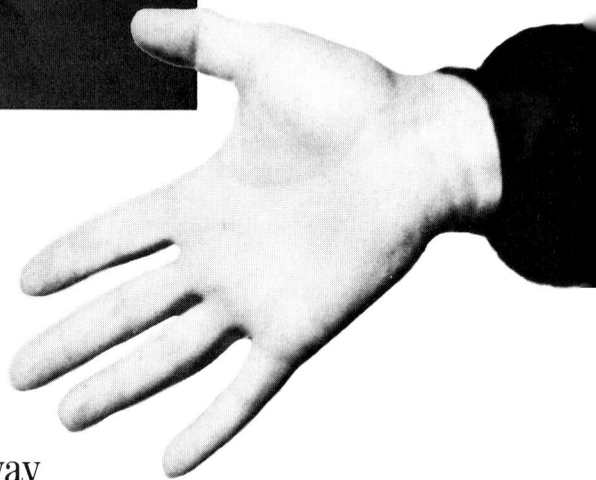

STAGE

FLYING HIGH

Sandy Duncan hit low points—two failed marriages and the loss of sight in one eye—between 1970's *The Boy Friend* and 1979's *Peter Pan,* when she soared again.

BIG NAME

"You're fired," said director Michael Bennett. "I quit," said Jennifer Holliday, who then came back and at 21 stole *Dreamgirls* with a heart-stopping solo about getting sacked.

DIANA WALKER

STAGE

NINE'S '10'

They started whistling at Anita Morris in sixth grade and by the time she was up-ended in her see-through costume in *Nine*, everybody cheered except TV viewers: censors nixed her act.

HEPCAT

Prowling, howling or prancing, the fantastic felines of Andrew Lloyd Webber's *Cats*—like Mr. Mistoffolees (Timothy Scot)—sang T.S. Eliot's furry verse to purrfection.

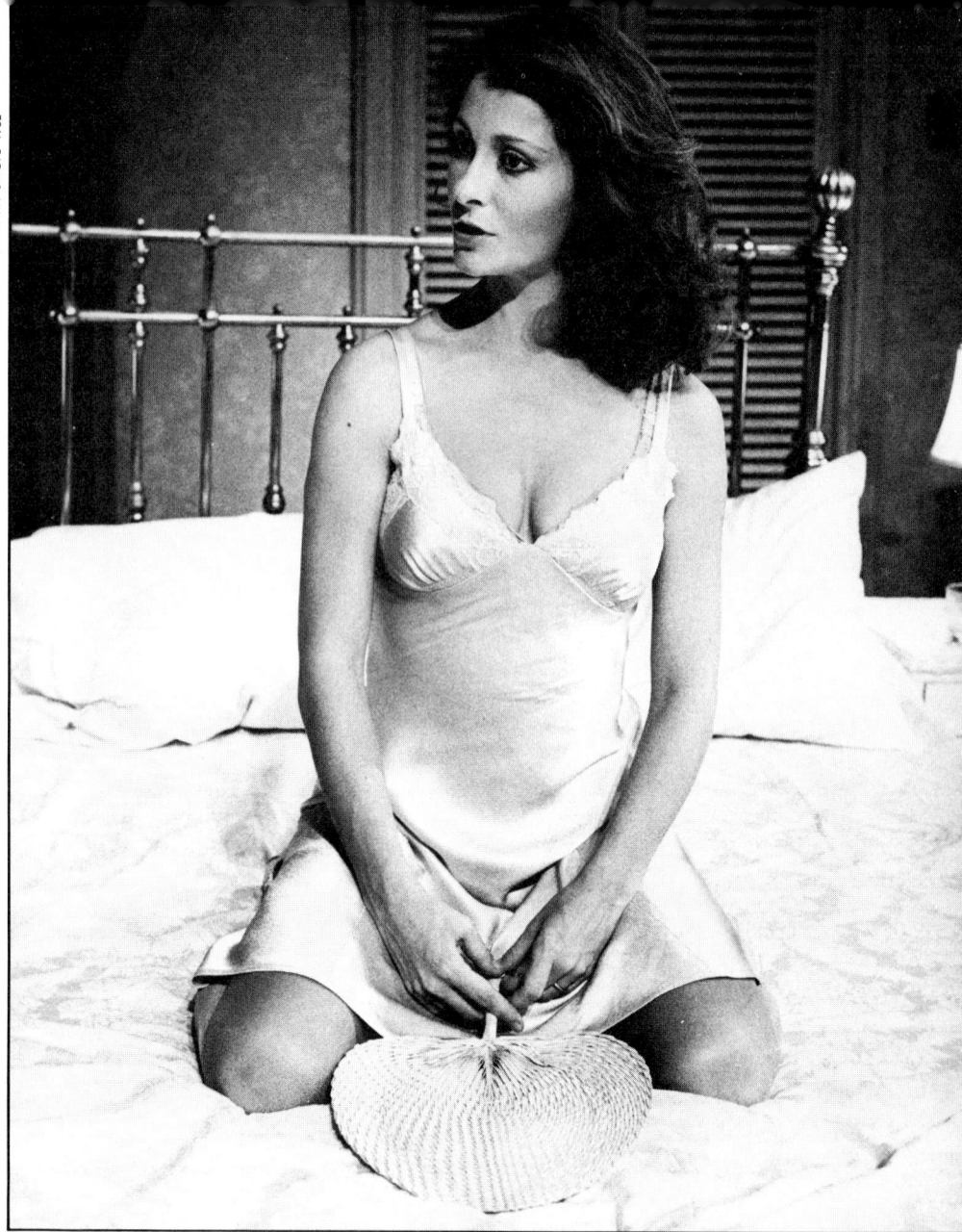

©MARTHA SWOPE 1982

HOT'S MAGGIE

Tennessee Williams called Elizabeth Ashley "the definitive Maggie" in the '74 revival of his *Cat on a Hot Tin Roof,* but the actress insisted, "I'm really just a trashy red-neck."

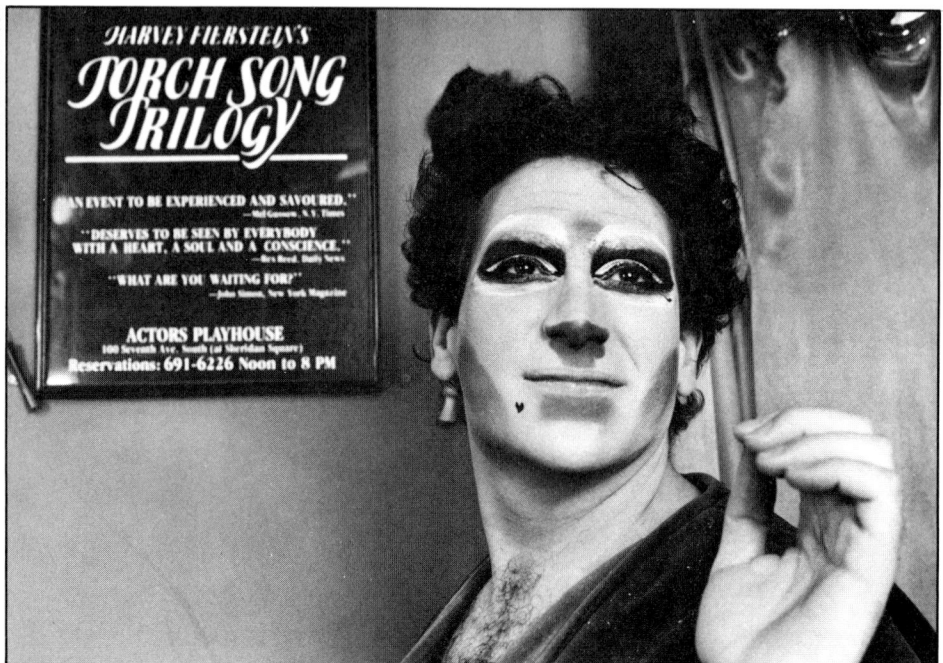

MICHAEL ABRAMSON/GAMMA-LIAISON

HARVEY FIERSTEIN'S
TORCH SONG TRILOGY

"AN EVENT TO BE EXPERIENCED AND SAVOURED."
—Mel Gussow, N.Y. Times

"DESERVES TO BE SEEN BY EVERYBODY WITH A HEART, A SOUL AND A CONSCIENCE."
—Rex Reed, Daily News

"WHAT ARE YOU WAITING FOR?"
—John Simon, New York Magazine

ACTORS PLAYHOUSE
100 Seventh Ave. South (at Sheridan Square)
Reservations: 691-6226 Noon to 8 PM

GAY TORCHBEARER

Highly uncloseted Harvey Fierstein wrote and starred in a sassy, moving drag-time comedy, reaped 1983 Best Play and Best Actor Tonys, and won the hearts of uneasy audiences.

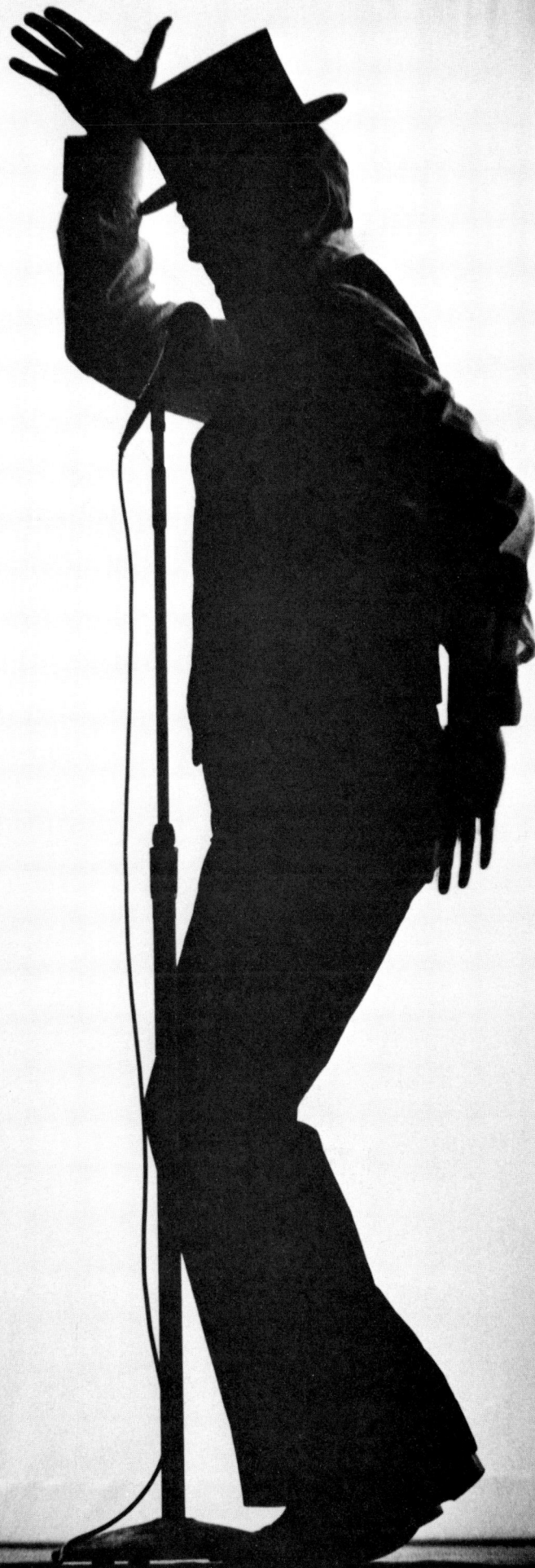

CABARET'S OLD CHUM

Lover of Edith Piaf, Marilyn Monroe and spouse Simone Signoret, Yves Montand at 60 went back to cabaret and brought down the house single-handedly.

Proving laughter is indeed the best medicine, Alan Alda's Hawkeye led the zany crew of *M*A*S*H* through 11 smash seasons of scalpel-sharp humor before the comedy series folded its tents in 1983.

BONNIE SCHIFFMAN

TUBE

HARRY BENSON

An oil-rich rascal named J.R., a squawk box known as Charlie and heroes with names like Hawkeye, Trapper John, Gonzo and the Fonz brightened the tube for millions of TV viewers. Miniseries drew maxi-audiences; daytime soaps, bolstered by sin and skin, inspired prime time imitators. The best of all this TV fare, whether sitcom or serious drama, seemed good from here to eternity. Re-runs, after all, can play forever.

ALL IN FUN

Carroll O'Connor showed his mug in 27 films and 120 TV shows before his debut as *All in the Family*'s Archie Bunker turned him into America's most famous fictive bigot.

MARY MOGUL

With her MTM Enterprises spinning out her weekly sitcom as well as *Rhoda* and *The Bob Newhart Show* in 1974, Mary Tyler Moore not only had the look, but was a TV tycoon.

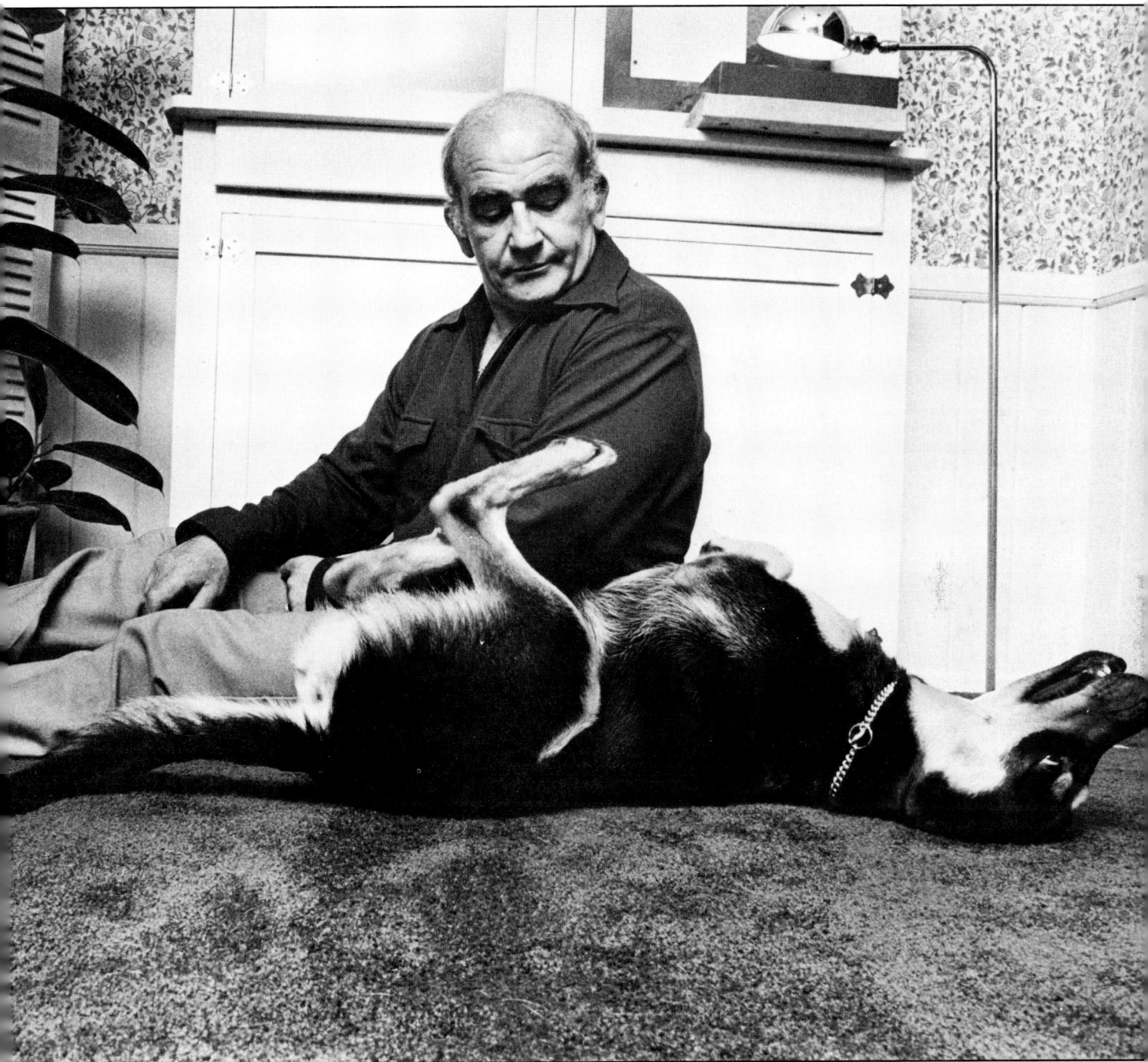

BELLY UP

Ed Asner thrived as curmudgeonly newsman Lou Grant for seven seasons on *The Mary Tyler Moore Show* and five more in his own spinoff before his series wound down.

TUBE

AAAAYY!

"TV put me here," exulted Henry Winkler, who was on top of the world in 1977 thanks to his *Happy Days* role as the Fonz and a movie lead in *Heroes*.

THREE'S COMPANY

His days as *The Waltons'* John-Boy done, Richard Thomas appeared next in 1981 in a real life domestic drama as the father of baby triplets.

©MIMI COTTER

172

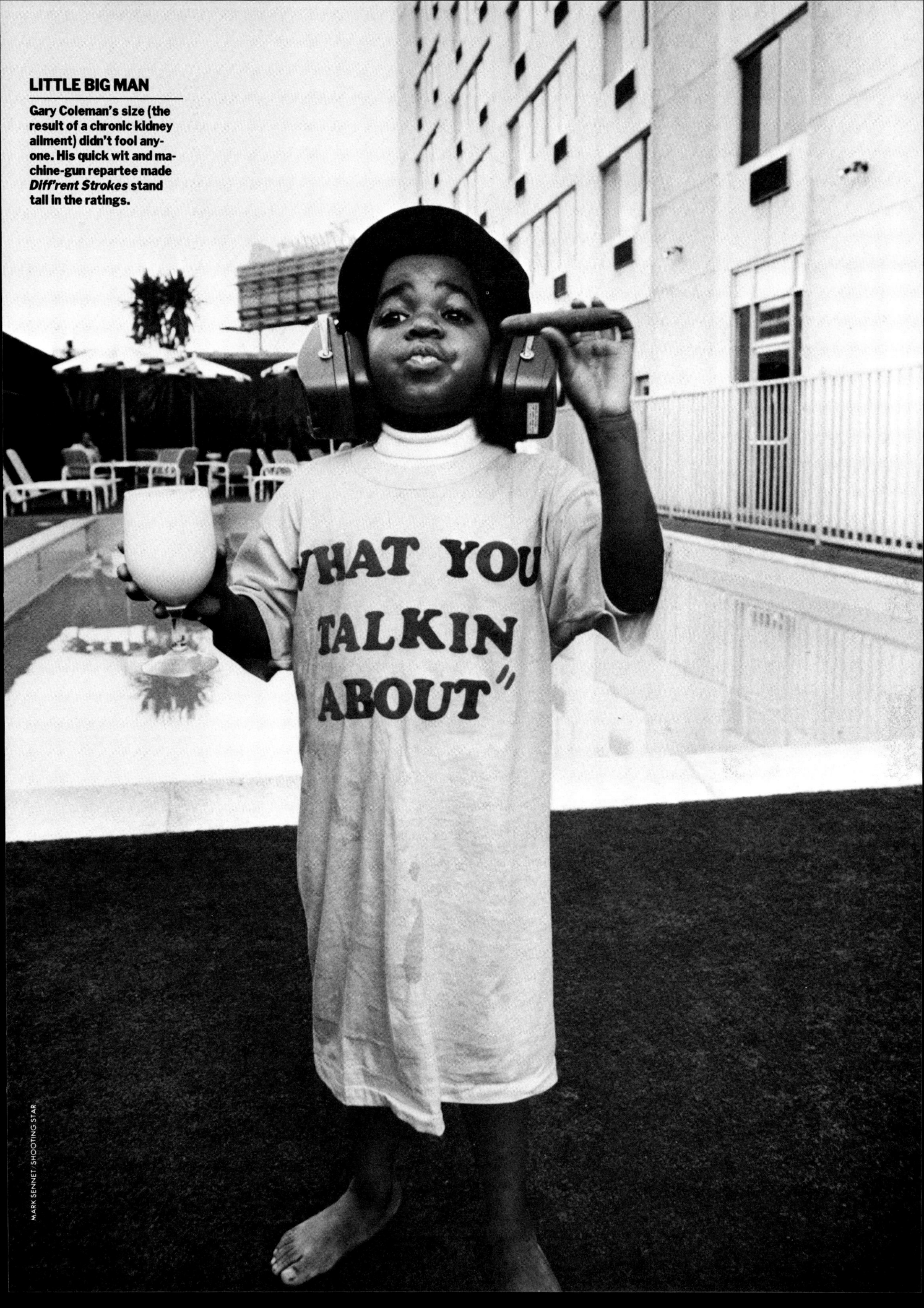

LITTLE BIG MAN

Gary Coleman's size (the result of a chronic kidney ailment) didn't fool anyone. His quick wit and machine-gun repartee made *Diff'rent Strokes* stand tall in the ratings.

MARK SENNET / SHOOTING STAR

TUBE

©STEVE SCHAPIRO

STUNNING SUB

South Dakotan Cheryl Ladd (shown with daughter Jordan) replaced fallen Angel Farrah in 1977 and spent four years in the series she jokingly dubbed "Chuck's Cherubs."

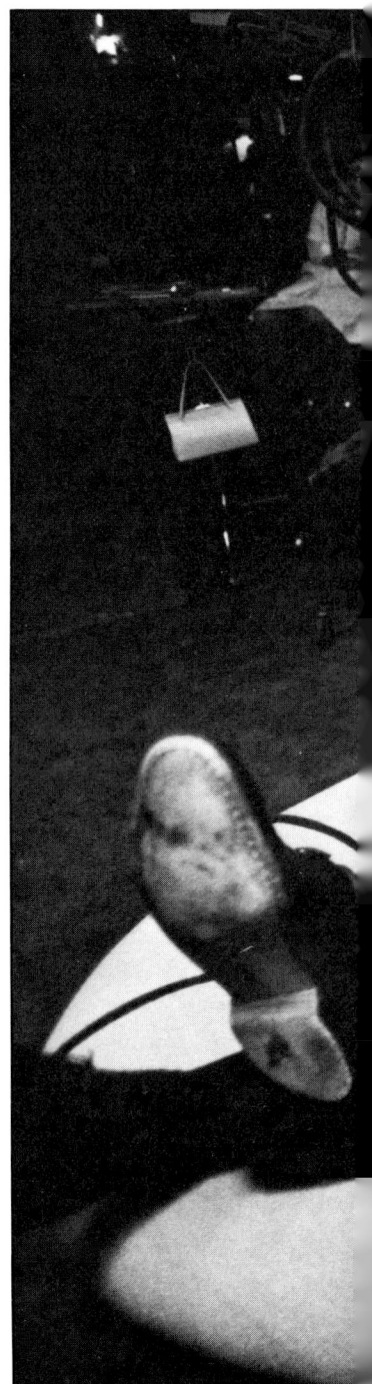

"People are ready for glamour on TV," concluded Farrah Fawcett in 1976 after *Charlie's Angels* with Jaclyn Smith (left), Kate Jackson (right) and David Doyle topped the ratings.

TUBE

GUESS WHO

J.R.'s shooting in 1980 didn't cripple *Dallas* ratings at all: They went through the roof as 35,625 PEOPLE readers voted on who did poor Larry Hagman in—and most guessed wrong.

SKATER DATER

Tony Geary's tough guy Luke produced a controversial rape on daytime TV. But when he finally married *General Hospital* co-star Genie Francis, even Liz Taylor did a cameo.

POT SHOTS

Black sitcoms got a boost from the hilarious Jeffersons. When Isabel Sanford, who played the wife, sashayed through the house trading barbs with husband George, fur flew.

MORKMANIA

Shifting from his *Mork & Mindy* TV role to movie stardom in *The World According to Garp* was "like going from Marvel Comics to Tolstoy," said Robin Williams in 1982.

HARRY BENSON

TUBE

A RARE CAT

"We all have to let go somehow. Silly is the great escape," proclaimed Steve Martin whose "wild and crazy guy" shtik was a regular delight on the *Tonight Show* and TV specials.

LIVE WIRE

Showing no shyness as a *Saturday Night Live* original, Gilda Radner tapped a mine of talent (and alter egos like Baba Wawa) to waltz off with a million laughs.

VALUABLE IMAGE

Barbara Walters' five-year, $5-million contract with ABC in 1976 threatened to make her a bigger star than many of the showbiz people she would later profile.

ARTHUR SCHATZ

RISING ANCHOR

"There are people smarter than I am, but nobody is going to outwork me," promised Dan Rather whose 110-hour-on-the-job weeks helped make him heir to CBS's Walter Cronkite in 1981.

NO SMALL TALK

Showing a sure hand as an interviewer (and with guests like the sperm-bank baby) Phil Donahue expanded his TV presence to morning *and* nighttime shows.

EVELYN FLORET

DALE WITTNER

KEN REGAN/CAMERA 5

HARRY BENSON

MODEST MACHO

Tom Selleck won the award as the Incredible Smirking Hunk for his detective series, *Magnum, P.I.* In private, he fended off dumb jock jokes with a fine sense of humor.

TOUGH COP

Dan Travanti usually got the best on *Hill Street Blues*: He whipped the bad guys, then he jumped into the sack with luscious co-star Veronica Hamel. Off camera, he finally licked a drinking problem.

TUBE

COOL HAND

Scoring big with two TV spectaculars, *Shōgun* and *The Thorn Birds*, Richard Chamberlain finally shed his *Dr. Kildare* image and proved himself a versatile actor—indeed, a man for all miniseries.

PLAY MISTY FOR
ME, OR ELSE

Isn't much in this game
Clint Eastwood hasn't
done—TV, pasta westerns,
producing, directing, his
own stunts. Oh yeah, and
the good ole California
boy is, at 53, still top
box office, too.

KEN REGAN/CAMERA 5

SCREEN

Into the limelight they came — discoing, boxing, dealing with every social and sexual problem under the sun and battling intergalactic ogres — a new supply of shiny, polymorphous stars, plus old favorites coming into their own.

186

WACKY WINNER

At 32 in 1978, Goldie Hawn (with first-born Oliver) had already hit in TV's *Laugh-In* **and garnered an Oscar for** *Cactus Flower*. **Then in 1980 came** *Private Benjamin*. **That's no mere ding-a-ling.**

HENRY WOLF

FASTEST LEGEND

Four years out of Yale Drama in '79 and looking like a cool goddess, Meryl Streep was on her way to four nominations and two Oscars (*Kramer vs. Kramer*** and ***Sophie's Choice***).**

HARRY BENSON

SMOKEY THE BARE

Making it look easy, perennial he-boy Burt Reynolds carried small movies on his back, gave us *Deliverance*, roamed untamed from Shore to Field, and posed nekkid, yet so far hasn't bagged an Oscar.

©ELLEN GRAHAM

WHEREFORE ART THOU?

He produced *Bonnie and Clyde*, co-wrote *Shampoo*, won a directing Oscar for *Reds* and starred in them all, but Warren Beatty may be best known for the company he didn't keep.

RING MASTER

Taking the *Rocky* road, Sly
Stallone won Best Movie
once and had three super-
hits. But still not satisfied,
he said in 1982 he hoped
to be reincarnated as the
heavyweight champ.

SCREEN

©STEVE SCHAPIRO

THE FLYING WHO?

For years after that dumb *Nun*, nobody loved Sally Field but the people, her kids (7 and 5 in 1977) and maybe Burt, but in 1979 her crisp, crusty *Norma Rae* won her an Oscar and overdue respect. Nice landing, sister.

WHAT PRICE ANGST?

Sprinting past the hoopla at a 1975 gala, sneaker-shod Woody Allen and Diane Keaton (they did *Annie Hall* together) seemed to have our times always, if shakily, in their grasp.

DO NOT CROSS
DEPT

POLICE DEPT.

SCREEN

NATURAL WONDER

"Just us girls," Jessica
Lange cooed of times with
her baby by Baryshnikov.
In 1983 the big girl, free
of *Kong*, set the world on
its ear with her lovely
art in *Frances* and *Tootsie*.

MARY ELLEN MARK/LEE GROSS

"She's 7 going on 29," reckoned director Steven Spielberg after Drew Barrymore, precocious granddaughter of the Great Profile, won audiences in *E.T.*

TONY COSTA

SCREEN

PUMPING IRONY

The grin is a jovial put-down, the pop eyes those of a rabbit pretending it's not there, and with them Eddie Murphy, after *SNL* and *Trading Places*, was making $1 million a picture at the age of 21.

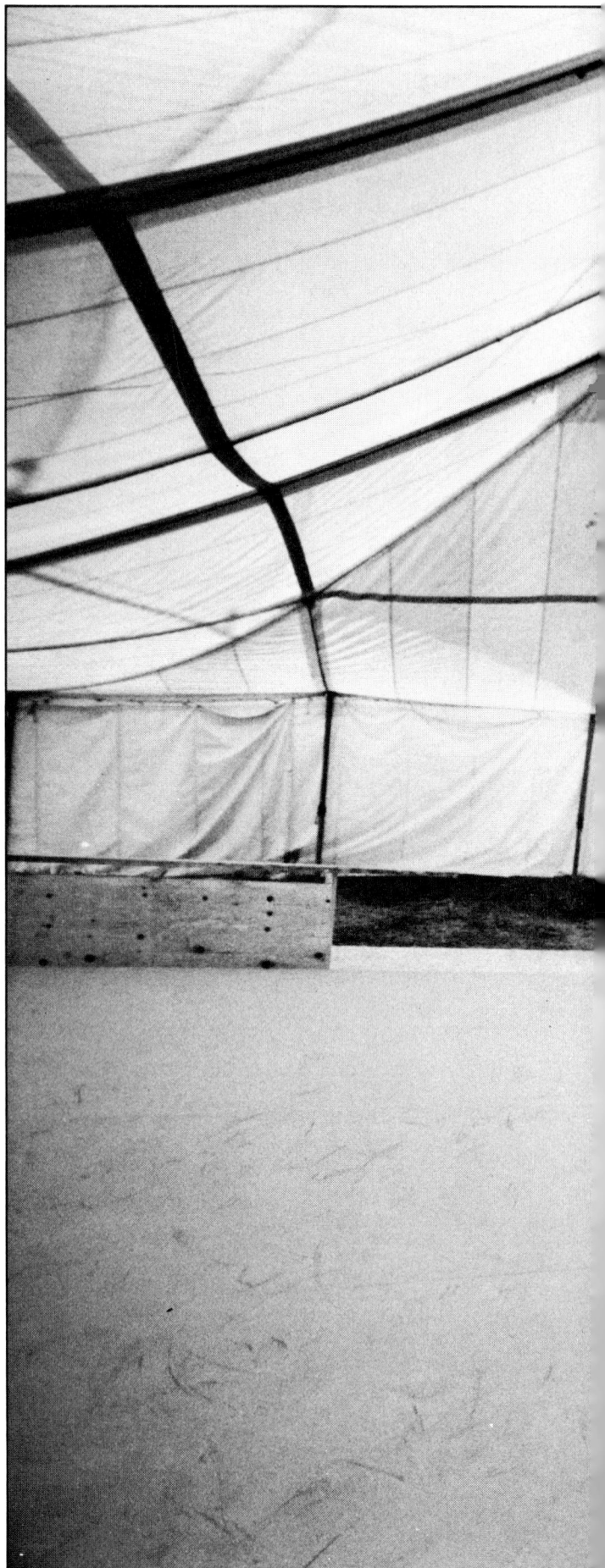

**ALIVE AND
KICKING**

Shaking with vanity, John
Travolta discoed from no-
where to the top in *Saturday Night Fever*, encored
in *Grease*, slipped, but was
back dancing in 1983's
Staying Alive.

195

DOGGED DUDLEY

His acting credits secured (*10* and *Arthur*), former jazz pianist Dudley Moore sat down in 1983 on the beach near his California home to prepare for a new class act, a debut at Carnegie Hall.

MARK SENNET/SHOOTING STAR

198

FORCESIGHT

Ah! R2-D2. Darth Vader. C-3PO. Leia. Luke Skywalker. Jabba the Hutt. Ewoks. All space childies of The Kid, George Lucas, 39. *Star Wars* ('77). *Empire* ('80). *Jedi* ('83). Six to go. Ah.

MAIN SQUEEZE

Ah-2. Steven Spielberg
made *Jaws* at 27, in 1975,
Close Encounters ('77),
Raiders (with Lucas in
'81), and *E.T.* ('82), whose
star Spielberg called "a
squashy little mensh."
Next?

SCREEN

"It's better if I don't go back to school right away," said Hope, awaiting the birth of her daughter. "We all need a chance to forget about this."

Patricia Hope

What are the rights of an unwed pregnant school teacher?

Most years, East Hampton, N.Y. High School has at least one unwed mother-to-be. Last fall there were two. "It's always nice having someone else who was going through the same thing," confides Patricia Hope, who is now eight months pregnant. "Between classes, when we'd see each other in the hallway and no one was looking, we'd compare stomachs." But unlike her expectant friend, Patricia Hope is not a student—she's a 41-year-old teacher.

To some residents of this fashionable Long Island resort (pop. 14,029), Hope is a heroine, a symbol of courage and rugged individualism. But to others she's the archetypal "fallen woman," a disgrace to both her sex and her profession. In November 1982, 19 East Hampton residents signed a petition accusing the biology and human behavior teacher of "immorality," and calling for her dismissal. "Her example certainly does not reflect the principles by which we feel teachers should live," it read.

In a nation where 191,073 unwed high school age girls gave birth in 1980, the concern was understandable, but far from universal. Hope's supporters retaliated with a petition signed by 469 parents, students and former students: "Pat Hope's genuine concern has made her

without question one of the most valuable teachers we are privileged to have teaching our youth. She is being unjustly judged, in that no one has the right to declare the morality or immorality of an individual."

The twice-divorced Hope, already the mother of a 20-year-old daughter, says she became pregnant because she wanted to have another child "before time ran out." She refuses to name the baby's father. "The relationship was a romantic dalliance," she says. "It ended before I found out I was pregnant."

That was not the case in 1980, when Hope became pregnant by a man with whom she was living. "We would have married if things had worked out," she says. During that pregnancy, school officials assigned her to an office job. But after 10 weeks, Hope miscarried and returned to her teaching post. Still, the school board called her in. "One member," Hope now recalls, "shook his finger at me and demanded, 'Don't ever do this again!'"

When she did, she provoked a storm that engaged the passions of East Hampton. "This should reawaken us to the immorality of the nation," exclaimed the Rev. Fred Jones, pastor of the Cedar Street Baptist Chapel. Hope's supporters rose to her defense. "It's her own business," said student Trisha Holmes. The school board agreed, after deliberation, that it would take no action against Hope. When she returns from a paid leave that began Dec. 22, she'll still have a job. Says Bob Freidah, the school superintendent, "Pat is a good teacher. She has promised me that the father is not a student. There's no reason to remove her from the classroom."

Hope's detractors see many reasons. Keeping her in school is "going against the values of

the family unit," said one. Superintendent Freidah explains that the emotional effect of a teacher's deportment on students is important. "The pregnancy did not affect her teaching," he notes. "She was in good health and only one parent threatened to remove her child from Pat's class." Had there been mass withdrawals, he adds, "the situation might have been different."

At the heart of the criticism of Hope's pregnancy, her supporters say, is that it's tangible evidence of illicit sex. Says one East Hampton father, "There is a male teacher at the high school who is having affairs with students. No one gets upset with him. Why? Because he doesn't have a big belly."

Many parents plainly worry that Hope's "indiscretion" is setting a bad example. Beatrice Steiner, whose daughter was in Hope's human behavior seminar, said she was appalled to

READERS SPEAK OUT
PEOPLE *asked those who read the Patricia Hope story to tell us how they would feel if a teacher in their school system were involved in the same situation.*
A high school teacher who becomes pregnant out of wedlock should be:
Dismissed **21%**
Reassigned **7**
No action should be taken.............................. **72**
A grade school teacher who becomes pregnant out of wedlock should be:
Dismissed **22%**
Reassigned **9**
No action should be taken.............................. **69**
A teacher who fathers a child out of wedlock should be:
Dismissed **21%**
Reassigned **6**
No action should be taken.............................. **73**

discover that the sensitive topic was being taught "by a woman about to deliver out of wedlock. Had we known, we never would have considered this course." Hope's Lamaze coach, Elizabeth Holmes, thinks such fears are ridiculous. "I'm the mother of a 16-year-old girl. A lot of her friends are sexually active. It's something I've regretfully learned to accept. If students are going to be promiscuous, it's not because of Pat."

Pat Hope knows the value of education; she had to struggle to get her own. The daughter of a journalist and a housewife, Pat, who was raised in Manhattan, married her high school sweetheart at 17. Their daughter, Hillary, now a sophomore at Clark University in Worcester, Mass., was born four years later. After the couple's divorce, Hope worked as a secretary, and attended college at night. In 1974, after getting her degree from Southampton College, she found her current job. She also joined a local theater group, the Spindrift Players, where she met and married an Irish actor. They were divorced within a year. "I'm a terrific teacher, director and mother," boasts Hope. "My only failures are in marriage."

While Hope awaits the birth of her baby girl—its sex disclosed by amniocentesis—she is living alone in a tiny room in an East Hampton rooming house, which she moved into to save money. But her biggest problem may begin when her daughter arrives. Then, Pat Hope must try to give the girl a normal childhood under the glaring eyes of a small town where, though yet unborn, she is already a celebrity.

January 17, 1983
By GIOIA DILIBERTO

Daughter Penelope Leigh Hope was born Feb. 5, 1983.

Anita Bryant

An All-American girl raises hackles invoking God vs. gays in Florida

For two decades Anita Bryant had combined her Miss America good looks (second runner-up, 1959) with a quintessentially American voice: clear, direct, untutored but unwavering. The result has been an American idyll: an itinerant, hand-to-mouth youth blossoming into devoted motherhood, riches and stardom. By 1977, the 37-year-old mother of four was earning $500,000 a year spreading the gospel of orange juice and sunshine on TV—and, in her inspirational books and records, the message of the Gospels as well. Then, Bryant says, she was summoned by God to a higher mission: to lead a crusade in Dade County, Fla., her home for 16 years, for the repeal of a new ordinance banning discrimination against homosexuals. To many old admirers, the voice of America had wandered off-key.

"If God had meant to have homosexuals," Anita declared, "he would have created Adam and Bruce." Reaching deep into her lexicon of Total Womanisms, biblical citations and warnings of Sodom-to-follow, she pushed the rhetoric of her crusade into overdrive. "If this referendum passes," she has said, "Dade County will have to hire known, flaunting homosexuals to teach our children ... Since homosexuals cannot reproduce, they must freshen their ranks with our children ... They will use money, drugs, alcohol, any means to get what they want ... This is a battle of the atheists and the ungodly on one side and God's people on the other."

Not surprisingly, the "ungodly" struck back—with T-shirts urging Miamians to "Squeeze a Fruit for Anita" and a proposed "gaycott" of products she advertises. Soon, however, pro-ordinance groups decided to let Anita do the talking. Says Jim Foster of the Dade County Coalition for Human Rights: "I'm confident that when any rational adult voter hears her, he will understand she is a mystic involved in irrational claims."

Such condescension aside, Anita has reason to be worried these days. She has received crank calls and bomb threats, and the post office now screens her mail. "It's kind of scary," says her husband and manager, Bob Green. "The police have asked us not to reveal where our children go to school." So far the Florida citrus growers have stuck by her, but the Singer sewing machine company has apparently suspended plans for a Bryant talk show. And it is not clear how long Anita will stay with her longtime booking agent, Richard Shack, whose wife, Dade County Commissioner Ruth Shack, introduced and supports the controversial ordinance. Bryant is troubled. "You couldn't have paid me a million dollars to do this if God hadn't called me," she says. "I'm ready to move away from Miami, if you want to know the truth."

Opponents fear she may do just that—transferring her crusade to other cities. Both sides see the Florida vote as a bellwether. "The issue," says rights coalition leader Ethan Geto, "is whether the Declaration of Independence, the Bill of Rights and the Constitution apply to some citizens only or to all." Bryant, who claims that the West Coast drought is heavenly retribution for a similar bill in California, believes otherwise. "There are no human rights when it comes to corrupting children," she contends. "I have seen the moral decay all around me—this kind of tolerance is wrong." Then she adds sorrowfully: "I used to think being a Christian meant living above the jungle. Now I know it means living *in* the jungle."

June 6, 1977

On June 7, the gay rights ordinance was repealed by a 2-1 vote. In 1980, Anita's Florida citrus contract ran out and she and Bob Green divorced. She moved to Selma, Ala. and opened a dress shop.

Before belting out *Battle Hymn of the Republic* at an antigay-rights rally, Bryant got a hand from cops. "It's God's battle, not mine," she said, but one critic claimed she spread "bigotry throughout the land."

Betty Friedan

Include men and the family, a founder urges the movement

In 1981, the 60-year-old founder and first president of the National Organization for Women questioned some of the tenets of the movement that she helped start with her 1963 manifesto, The Feminine Mystique. *In* The Second Stage *(Summit Books, $14.95), Friedan vigorously argued that feminism's antipathy to the values of heart and hearth was causing a "backlash" and dooming the Equal Rights Amendment. Divorced from an ad man since 1970, she described her relationship with her grown children, Daniel, a physicist, Jonathan, an engineer, and Emily, a medical student, as being now "better than ever." Friedan spoke candidly with assistant editor Bonnie Johnson of* PEOPLE *about the current stage of women's—and men's—liberation.*

What is wrong with the women's movement today?

We're very much in danger of getting locked into a "feminist mystique" that will deny us a part of our personhood just as much as the feminine mystique did. Listening to my daughter and to her generation, I sensed something was not getting to them right. They're working so hard at their careers, and they are trying not to be trapped like their mothers were. But underneath I find that there's increasing bitterness, pain and an unspoken accusation: "You people have saddled us with these difficult goals. Now what

are we supposed to do with our other needs?"

So jobs haven't brought fulfillment?

No. As things are structured, women find they can't "have it all." They're trying to run homes and families by standards that were set by women who had to find their whole status and power in their domestic roles. I call it female machismo. They're also trying to perform outside jobs up to standards set by men who had wives to take care of all the details of life. But I find these females do not like the idea of being superwomen.

What has to change?

For one thing, we have to include men and work with them, not against them, to cast new roles that are less confining to both sexes. The women's movement has gone as far as it can with women alone.

But many women are still turned off by the movement. Why?

Women whose whole identity is bound up with the family have felt threatened. It seemed like we were condescending to them and disdained everything they stood for. The family is important to me and to every feminist. There is a false polarization between feminism and the family which the right wing and the Moral Majority are hypocritically manipulating. If we don't affirm equally our new personhood in society and the part of us that is just as basic—the love and nurturing of children—then feminism will take another 50 years to succeed.

You've been accused of abandoning your cause. How do you respond?

I'm making no 180-degree turn. I never thought that men

were the enemy. And I always knew there is no win for women when you pit marriage and motherhood against a career. It's an impossible choice.

What should be done?

First, we have to recognize that the family is not just a buzzword for reactionaries. In all its varied forms it may be critical for our survival. To strengthen the family and make child rearing a realistic choice, we need maternity and paternity leaves, flexible scheduling of work hours, shared jobs, good child-care programs and possibly tax rebates for people who assume primary responsibility for raising a child. I also think that we might consider taking some of those workers—male and female—who have been laid off by the major industries and retraining them for careers in child care.

November 16, 1981

The divorced Friedan (in her Manhattan apartment where she lived alone) urged both sexes to transcend "feminist rhetoric," but critic Ellen Willis charged that she "would destroy feminism in order to save it."

Brigitte Bardot

A French sex kitten's crusade to save seals gets iced-up in Newfoundland

Each spring hunters at the remote Canadian outpost of St. Anthony, Newfoundland, venture out on the ice to kill baby harp seals: The trusting animals are bludgeoned, then skinned for their pelts. Animal lovers the world over have condemned the slaughter—in 1977 the predicted kill was 170,000—and a group of protesters flew to the scene, among them actress Brigitte Bardot, then 42. This account is from her diary:

Taking off from Paris, I feel frightened, as always. Here we are squashed in with the baggage, with 14 hours flying ahead.

Stopping off in Reykjavik, Iceland, I call Paris. My housekeeper says French President Giscard d'Estaing just called, wanting to talk to me about the baby seals. Too bad. I would love to explain my feelings.

Hours later we fly over the ice fields where the hunters will be killing helpless baby seals tomorrow. A rage swells up inside me. I think about these poor little creatures who live so peacefully, with no defense against attackers. I feel sick.

The next day, in Quebec, I call Paris. Wonderful news! President Giscard d'Estaing's secretary has just rung up saying the government will prohibit the importation of sealskins.

But the Canadian journalists interview me as though I were promoting a film, and our arrival in St. Anthony the next day is terrifying. Reporters there accuse me of wearing sealskin. I am asked if I eat meat. I respond in my broken English that if I eat meat, it is to survive— sealskins keep no one alive. The journalists mock me, nudging each other and laughing. I can't stand this any more.

Later I try to pull myself together for another press meeting, but my hair has lost its body, my eyes have circles under them, and my clothes are crumpled. It's like being at war. But a strength rises in me. I look them in the face and say shut up. I am not here for fun, and I am speaking for the entire world. "In Europe," I say, "you are called 'Canadian assassins.' " There is a frosty silence, then agitation.

The next day we try to reach the ice fields. It is 20 degrees below zero (centigrade). Snow falls. Our helicopter pilot can't see anything. We are thrown about, the wind so strong we have to shout. I am numb with fear. It would be so silly to die like this. But now a miracle! Suddenly I see tents at a volunteer camp below.

The next day we make our last try. The skies clear and all of a sudden I see seals—babies covered in white fur, like little balls of yarn. I feel like laughing and crying. The helicopter drops us off on the ice. The baby seals look at us confidently with their big, soulful eyes. I take one in my arms, kiss his wet nose and my tears join his. Suddenly the mother appears, and her cries beckon the baby. She gives me a quizzical look, discovering me kissing her baby. Could she be jealous? I'm sorry, Mama Seal, but I will spend my life fighting for him.

April 11, 1977

BB got to this baby harp seal before hunters did, and soon after hostile local reporters got to her.

Wilma Wilson

Faced with his terminal cancer, a couple makes a courageous choice

They became hand-holding sweethearts in high school after she playfully pushed him into the swimming pool one day, and they got married seven years later. Don Wilson was easygoing, fun-loving and "all man," and in their 31 years of marriage, says Wilma Wilson, now 54, that never changed. "We did everything together."

Then last July Don, 55, a tall, strong plumber who lived in the Detroit suburb of Mount Clemens, complained of a urinary problem. Wilma accompanied him to the hospital, where doctors found a large cancerous tumor in his bladder. "It doesn't look good," a physician told the couple. "In fact, it looks bad." When he left the hospital briefly after 13 days of treatment, Don told his wife: "I don't want a lot of stuff hooked up to me. I'm telling you now, if things get worse I want you to cut the treatments."

And things got worse. Finally, after months of soul-searching, Wilma, her son, Curtis, 25, and daughter-in-law, Ruth Ann, decided to cut off the intravenous support systems that had been keeping Don alive for the past few weeks. "It was not an easy decision," she says, struggling to hold back her tears. "Do we let him go on or do we let him have some peace? I watched him suffer for seven months. That was enough. I knew I had to make a decision—right or wrong." Don Wilson left Cottage Hospital in Grosse Pointe and now is at the Hospice of Southeastern Michigan in Southfield, where all the patients are terminally ill.

Was Wilma Wilson's decision correct? Do people have "the right to die"? Who may decide if a dying patient should be granted a quick and peaceful death? Who, for that matter, decides what death is? And if doctors withhold extraordinary treatment from the terminally ill, should they be prosecuted for murder?

In March 1983, after a two-year study, the President's Commission for the Study of Ethical Problems in Medicine and Biomedical and Behavioral Research recommended that when death looms as a certainty, a mentally competent and fully informed patient should be allowed to halt the treatment that keeps him alive. If a patient is incapable of making such a decision, the commmission suggested, the family then should be permitted to take that responsibility.

The report, while not binding, may at last provide hospital authorities and families with some workable guidelines. Experts estimate that 80 percent of all Americans now die in health care institutions, and, according to commission chairman Morris B. Abram, most of them do not have formal policies to deal with right-to-die problems. "The reigning principles today are the fear and trembling that surround those decisions," says Abram, a New York City lawyer and former president of Brandeis University. "The fear is that the patient's loved one may be doing something that's final. The trembling is that the loved one may be doing something that is not legal." Moreover, fears of prosecution or malpractice suits can inhibit doctors and hospitals from carrying out a dying patient's wishes.

The absence of clear-cut policies has brought the courts more and more into medical matters that were once the province of patient and doctor alone. In a landmark 1976 ruling, the New Jersey Supreme Court allowed the parents of comatose Karen Ann Quinlan to disconnect her from a life-sustaining respirator. Quinlan defied medical odds and last week reached her 29th birthday; still comatose, she survives in a northern New Jersey nursing home, receiving nourishment through a tube. In California last month, a municipal judge dismissed murder charges against two doctors who had stopped life support, including nourishment, to a severely brain-damaged man. A New York Supreme Court justice ruled in favor of a crippled diabetic patient who had demanded that his hospital halt dialysis and other life-sustaining treatments and allow him to go home to die.

Ironically, while the Abram commission was reporting its findings, the Reagan Administration published new and binding regulations denying federal funds to any hospital that deprives care to handicapped newborns. These rules probably are a consequence of last year's "Baby Doe" incident in Bloomington, Ind. In that case, parents and their doctors agreed not to perform corrective surgery on a baby born with Down's syndrome. Before the infant died, an Indiana court upheld the parents and doctor.

Such scattered court decisions and the Abram report will not end the right-to-die controversy. State legislatures across America, for example, are debating so-called natural death bills. These would permit a person to sign a "living will," stating that he does not want his life prolonged artificially after a physician says there is no hope for recovery. So far 15 states have passed such laws. Advocates say that every person is entitled to "die with dignity," while opponents claim that these laws will invite mercy killing and infanticide.

Ultimately, public debate is overwhelmed by private grief, and that is something that cannot be legislated. "Nobody gives you a crash course on what to do when someone is dying," says Wilma Wilson. She vividly recalls an early visit that she made to her husband in the hospital. "He was in the cancer patient area and this jolly nurse came up to me with this little brochure on hospices about dying with dignity. I was furious. I think I could have hit her. We weren't in here to die!

RIGHT TO DIE

PEOPLE *asked those who read the story about Don and Wilma Wilson what they felt about the rights of the dying and their families.*

Should a terminally ill patient have the right to refuse medical treatment that would prolong his or her life?

Yes	99%
No	1

If the patient is not competent to make such a decision, should the family have the legal right to do so?

Yes	98%
No	2

If you had to decide whether such treatment should continue or stop, what would you do?

I would continue treatment	2%
I would stop it	95
Don't know	3

been so robust suffer such excruciating pain. After consulting with her family and Don's four doctors, it was agreed that Wilson should be taken off his life-support system. "Even now I wonder if I made the right decision," Wilma says. Some of her friends were shocked. "How could you let him die?" one demanded. "God, if they could see him down from 190 to 118 pounds," Wilma says. "He'd had enough."

If there is any solace for Wilma and her family, it is that her husband has been comfortable at the hospice, untethered, and receiving large doses of morphine and drugs to offset nausea and pain. In fact, last week he was actually savoring his final days. "I felt like I didn't care," he recalled of the time before he came to the hospice. "I didn't want to wake up. I had cancer and wasn't getting better. Why try?" Now, although he quit cigarettes nine years ago, he is smoking up to a pack a day and, ignoring his history as a diabetic, nibbling on sweets.

And every day Wilma, of course, is there, running her fingers through his hair, kissing his forehead and holding his hand, just as she did in all of those past years together. "When you live with someone 31 years," she says, "you know what they want. Even though I know he's close to death, at least I feel like he's back among the living."

April 11, 1983
Written by CAROL WALLACE
and reported by JULIE
GREENWALT

Don Wilson succumbed to cancer as the above story was going to press. His family stayed together with him in the hospice through the last night. "We would not change one thing we did," said his son, Curtis. "It was perfect."

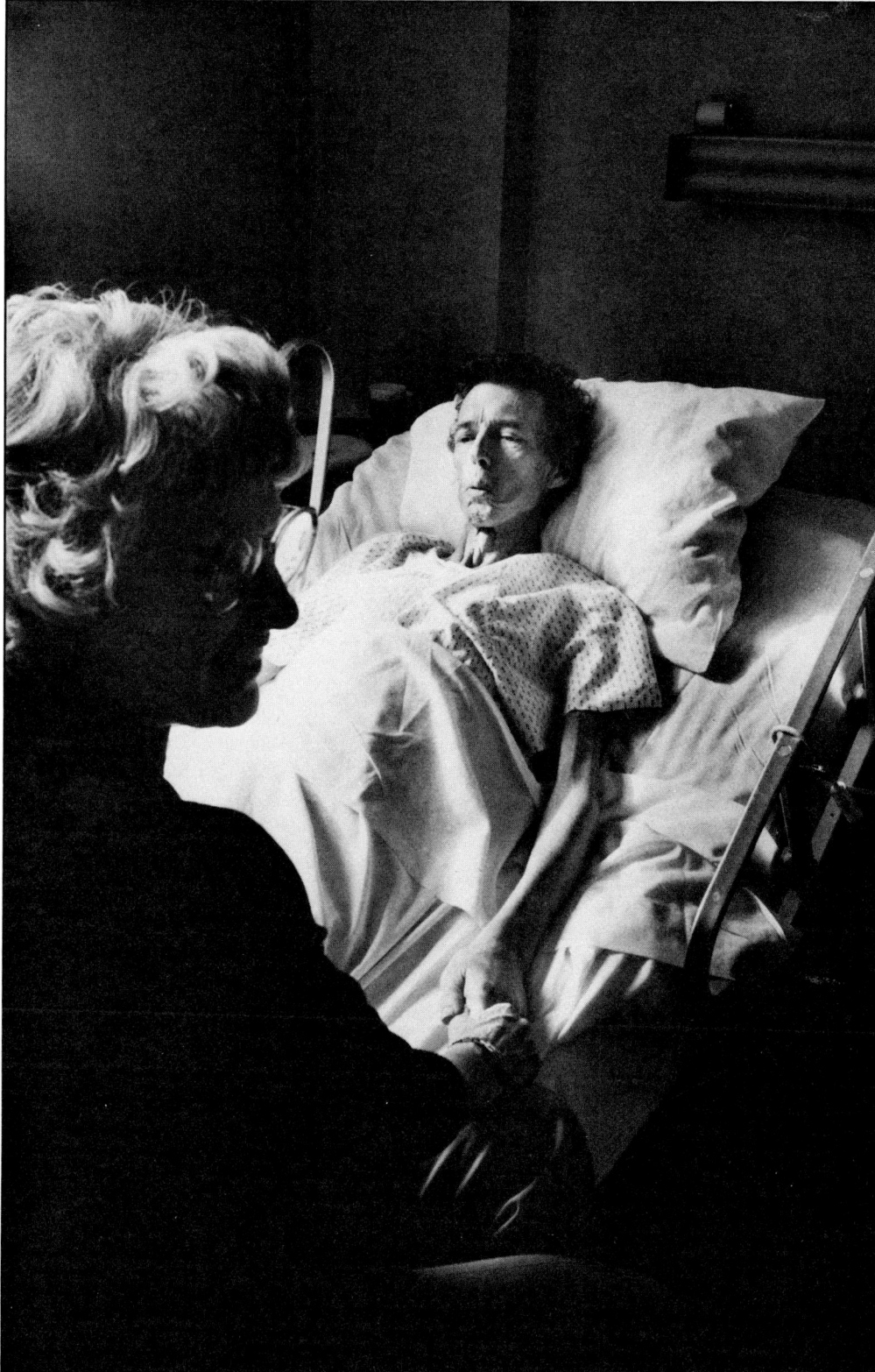

Wilma Wilson's strength buoyed the spirits of her husband, Don, but he refused to talk about death. "It would be better if he could," said Wilma, "but he just can't."

Don was in here to get treatment and get well! I took the pamphlet home and tore it into 16 pieces."

But her husband did not get well. Finally, after three major operations, extensive chemo-therapy and a month of radiation treatment, Don's doctors told him and his family they felt that nothing more could be done for him. (The hospital bill totaled about $35,000.)

"Well," said Don, "if you can't do anything, I don't want you to prolong it." But the instinct to do "everything possible" overrode his wishes. He was hooked up for another five weeks until Wilma could no longer bear to watch the man who had always

Song

MAIL EGOS

Gene Simmons and Kiss fused heavy metal and heavier makeup to prove in the '70s that mail-order marketing could reap millions.

The '70s was music's Gilded Age, as rock, country, disco, punk and pop turned purveyors of hype and hip into corporate colossi. The recession and the industry's urge to survive it forged a New Music for the '80s: pared-down, high-tech—and geared for the video revolution.

GYPSY LADY

Her writhing and haunting ballads, such as *Rhiannon* and *Sara*, put Stevie Nicks at the visual and vocal core of Fleetwood Mac. In the '80s she has soared also as a solo act.

HEAT WAVE

Linda Ronstadt was rock's First Lady in the '70s, but credit her torrid pipes on LPs like *Heart Like a Wheel*, not her fabled romance with California's Gov. Jerry Brown.

ROCK OF SAGES

Bob Dylan's low-budget Rolling Thunder tour in 1975 foreshadowed rock's New Wavenomics—but hardly his later embrace of Christ. Many fans preferred the Gospel according to Old Dylan.

KEN REGAN/CAMERA 5

SOULED OUT

Innervisions got Stevie Wonder to *Higher Ground*; *Songs in the Key of Life* put him into commercial orbit in 1976. Those masterworks earned the genius of soul-pop 15 Grammys in the '70s.

JOHN OLSON

Song

FEET ACCOMPLI

Elton John embodied pure flash in the pantheon of pop with an endless string of hits. Still, Captain Fantastic said in 1975 he'd also "like to be singles champ at Wimbledon."

SATIN DOLLS

The Bee Gees hit their peak on the *Saturday Night Fever* LP in 1977 (15 million sold so far). Then the kings of blue-eyed R&B lost their stripes on a *Sgt. Pepper* film/LP debacle.

213

Song

WINNER BY MILES

Miles Davis' horn led in be-bop, cool and fusion jazz, then he was stilled for five years by polyps, a hip implant and more. When he blew in again, in 1981, it seemed as though he'd never been away.

215

Song

**PARTON'S
SWEET SORROW**

She took the bus to Nash-
ville right after high school
and, a high-wigged idol at
31, sadly rode away from
country in 1977 to bust
into pop, after which Dolly
Parton was tough to top.

HARRY BENSON

216

WRITES THE SONGS, ALSO

His voice made molasses seem acrid but his jingles (Pepsi) and singles (*Mandy*) made Barry Manilow a family pet by 1977. "I'm only a fair singer but a great arranger," he said.

KEN REGAN/CAMERA 5

AMERICAN BIRDS

The only made-in-the-USA group flying high in 1975, the Eagles' laid-back rock earned $350 million before, shot up by dropouts and hell raising, they flew apart in 1980.

217

WILLIE THE FIRST

Once they finally started listening, it took stubborn, road-loving Willie Nelson no time at all to twang his way from crazy outlaw to country lord, having captured stardust on the way.

SHELLY KATZ/BLACK STAR

MARK SENNET/SHOOTING STAR

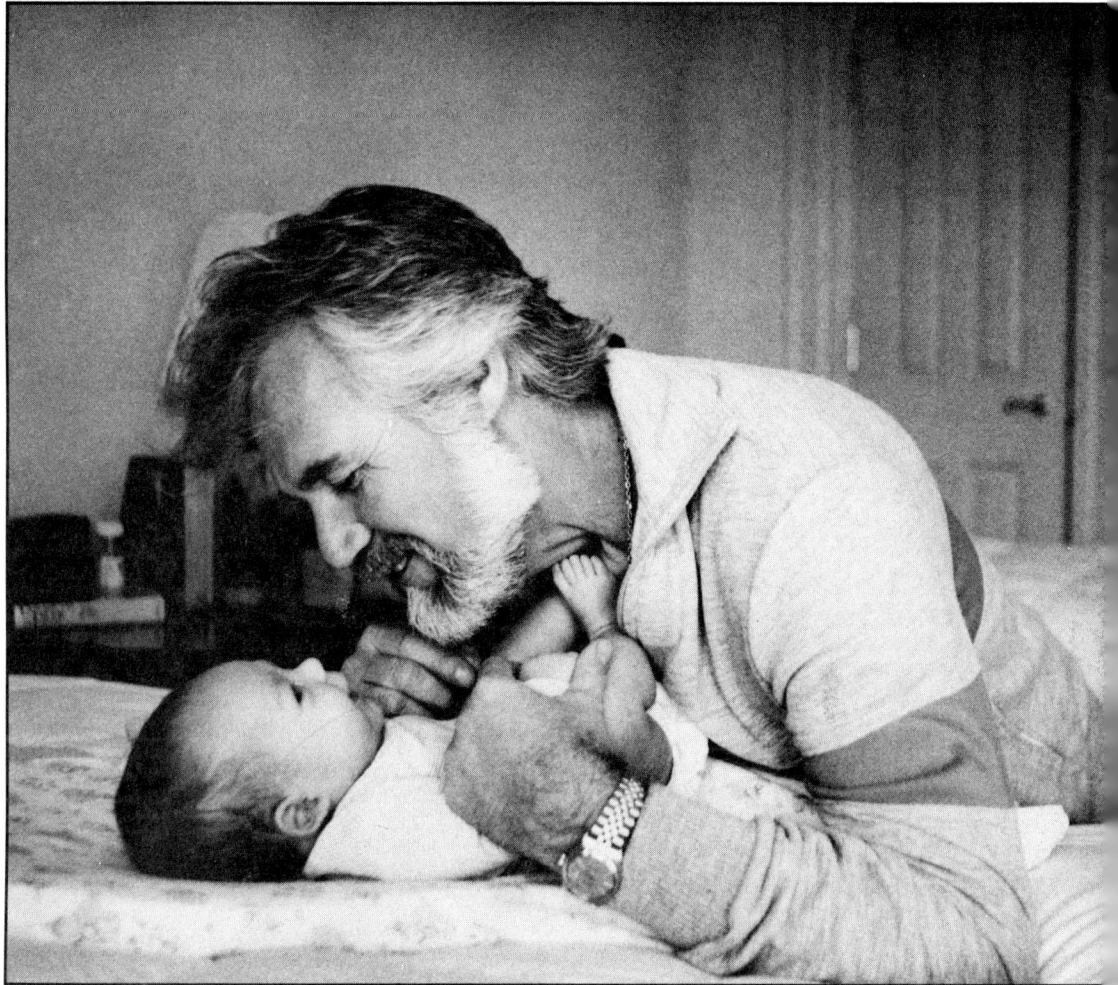

ROYALTY FLUSH

Although hits like *The Gambler* had helped push Kenny Rogers toward the $2 million-a-month income bracket, his biggest treasure in 1982 was newborn son Cristopher Cody.

WILD ABOUT HARRY

"I'm an escape artist," said Debbie Harry, reful- gent in minis and with the best come-hither pout since MM—and presto! her warbling sent Blondie's sales outasight.

Song

TORRID SUMMER

It was a long way from her first church solo at 10, but *Love to Love You Baby,* the nearly 17-minute scorcher by Donna Summer, heated up the charts for 14 weeks in 1978-79.

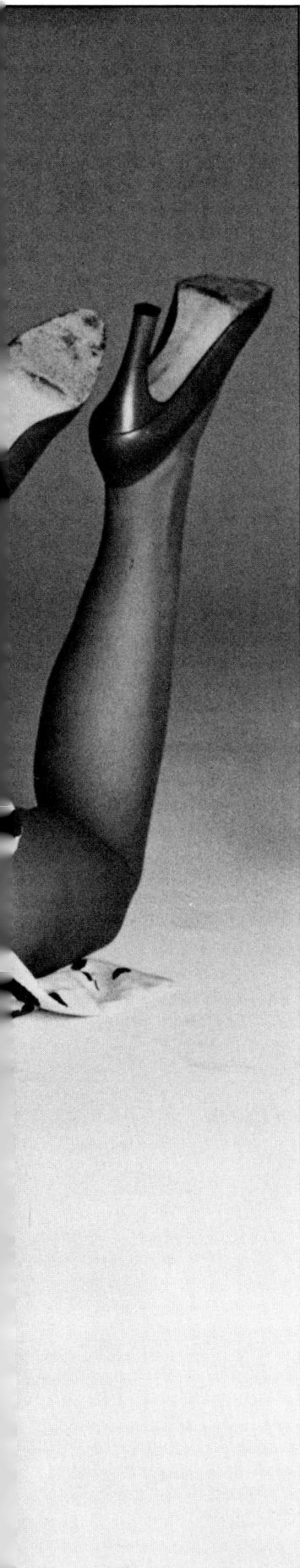

©1983 JULIAN WASSER

221

JOCK ROCK

Her sugary country-pop sound helped define that slick, mellow genre in the '70s; but Olivia Newton-John sizzled when she got *Physical* for an '82 Grammy-winning TV clip.

NEAL PRESTON/CAMERA 5

POLICE STATE

With their rhythmically intricate, melodically inventive fusion of reggae and pop, the Police stormed out of London to become the finest New Music band of the '80s.

Song

THRILLER

Michael Jackson fled the family act, did *The Wiz*, then roared off on his own to become a charismatic new '80s superstar. His dazzling dance routines for MTV clips conveyed his message: *Don't Stop 'Til You Get Enough*.

PETER C. BORSARI

MADDY MILLER

POP'S TOP PAIR

No pop duo since Simon and Garfunkel bagged more hits than Hall & Oates. Despite a fondness for things medieval, their lyrical, driving style on hits like *Maneater* delivered state-of-the-art pop-rock craftsmanship.

STILL ALOFT

As singer for Led Zeppelin, Robert Plant was *the* voice of heavy metal through the '70s. Since the band's demise, Plant has kept Zep's spirit and energy alive as a solo artist.

225

COPING

After near-fatal illness, an actress faces the death of a marriage

Her acting credits included a Broadway Tony (for Another Part of the Forest*), a 1964 Oscar (for* Hud*) and enough meaty roles to make any modern starlet wince with envy. Yet for Patricia Neal, born in 1926, real life provided the most tragic of dramas. Seven years after her 1953 marriage to British writer Roald Dahl (*Kiss, Kiss; Charlie and the Chocolate Factory*), Neal found herself struggling with the rehabilitation of their young son, Theo, who had been hit by a New York taxi. (Theo survived, but with mild brain damage.) The couple later lost a daughter, Olivia, to measles, and in 1965 Neal herself, then pregnant with their fifth child, suffered strokes that left her comatose for two weeks and threatened to destroy her powers of speech. Thanks to Dahl's encouragement, she recovered to give birth to daughter Lucy, now 17, and eventually resumed her career in films and television. By 1983 she had a lucrative contract as the Anacin "Fight pain and win" advocate in commercials. But while she was filming an earlier TV commercial for Maxim coffee, Neal had met a wardrobe woman, now in her mid-40s, who soon became a family friend, frequent houseguest and—Neal lamented—a secret rival for Dahl's affection. She has refused to identify the woman. Neal, prior to her divorce from her husband of 30 years, moved into her own retreat on the island of Martha's Vineyard. There she gave an account of her most recent setback to Mary Fischer for* PEOPLE.

So many horrendous things have happened to me, but that our marriage has not worked is the most agonizing. I just can't swallow it. It's as if the worst dream I can think of has happened. During my stroke our relationship was very good. Those were terrible times, but my husband pushed me to get well. He's really the one who did it. He pushed me to go to a military hospital for exercises and swimming, and he pushed me back into acting. I had no confidence at all after the stroke, but my husband insisted. He had married an actress, and he thought it would be good for me. I'm so very glad he did, because now it's all I've got.

He met his lady friend nine years ago. She was from a nice home, had been married and had three daughters. It's horrible looking back on how many times we were all together on holiday and I never knew. I took her into my home for a couple of weeks after she had been hospitalized. My eldest daughter, Tessa, was always very fond of her, and my son, Theo, had a crush on one of her daughters. Once she was at my house, and we were having a girl talk together. She told me about her new love, a married man with one son and three daughters. "Oh," I said at the time, "that's just like Roald and me."

Being her friend, I wanted happiness for her and asked whether her lover would ever leave his wife for her. "He'd like to," she told me. "He doesn't love her." Of course she was talking about Roald right to my face, and I didn't know it. Oh, it was ghastly.

I didn't know about the affair for a year and a half, and then I found out one night while all three of us were at a London gambling casino. She and I were on our way to the ladies' room when she turned and for 15 seconds gave me a look that said, "I've got him. You've lost him. To hell with you." My heart went to my head and back. When I confronted my husband, he admitted it but let me think the affair was over. I should have known better, but I didn't want to. I'd loved him for many years, and to me, when you get married, you're married forever.

When I think about it now, though, the marriage got worse over the years he was seeing this woman, and I guess I was just crazy to have tried to keep it going. I was an idiot. He's a killer with women, and he wanted to get rid of me years ago. He's the one who encouraged, almost demanded that I buy a house on Martha's Vineyard three

On a harbor dock in Edgartown, Martha's

years ago. That way I'd be far from him and his lady friend in England.

Two years ago last December, I learned the affair was still going on—when my daughter Ophelia told me so in England, in the presence of my husband. He had asked her to tell me. I don't give up easily, but it became a matter of pride and I finally left. At the airport, when my daughter Lucy was saying goodbye, my husband was laughing his head off over something. This whole thing is agonizing to me as a woman, and it's damaged my self-confidence. I blame both my husband and the woman, and I will always be furious with them.

Life can be tough, it really can, and I don't know what tomorrow's going to be like. But I refuse to sit around on Martha's Vineyard and brood. I have great friends who have been very kind to me. I love to act, and I would love to have a great film. I'm scouting for work now. I travel, give lectures on how I've overcome the difficulties in my life. I'm very busy. And I just bought a gorgeous apartment in New York that looks out over the East River. I suppose, though, I've found the greatest peace in something I do about four times a year, and that's going on a retreat at a convent in Connecticut. They're very kind there, and it's just beautiful.

Helen Keller once wrote that when one door of happiness closes, another opens. But often we look so long at the closed door that we don't even see the one that has opened for us. We must all find our lives as beautiful as God intended. So now I'm going to begin my life all over again. I just hope it's going to be good.

June 27, 1983

Vineyard, Patricia Neal contemplated a future alone in a house that's comfortable but seemed too lonely.

COPING

A paralyzed soprano sings a song of success

BY BARBARA ROWES AND
SARAH MOORE HALL

No one doubted that Irene Gubrud could sing. The 34-year-old lyric soprano was, after all, a winner in 1980 of the prestigious Naumburg Competition. The question as she made her operatic debut in 1981 in St. Paul, Minn., was whether Gubrud, whose legs have been partially paralyzed since childhood, could move about the stage through four grueling acts of Puccini's *La Bohème*. She answered with a performance that brought an audience of 1,700 to their feet cheering.

"This is something I've wanted for as long as I can remember," Gubrud enthused afterward. Though she has established a much-acclaimed recital career, grand opera had always been closed to her. "But I

**"I can't watch life through a closed door,"
concluded Gubrud, who hit the high notes
at a concert in Purchase, New York.**

was determined," she says. "Opera is meat and potatoes for a singer." Finally the year-old Opera St. Paul gave the Minnesota-born performer a chance. "We're a small, new company," says director Virginia Hardin Olson, "so we can be flexible."

Gubrud first heard opera on the radio in Canby, Minn., where as a toddler she used to stand on the kitchen table and sing along with the arias. The youngest of four children and only daughter of an electrician, she took up the flute at 9. Four years later, when her safety belt snapped on the Loop-O-Plane at a county fair, she was thrown to the concrete. She suffered smashed vertebrae and a damaged spinal cord, but after three months in a body cast, she resumed flute practice in a wheelchair.

"Music was a liberation from my body," explains Gubrud, who won a statewide competition within six months of the accident. "It was the one area where I could be free." Later, at Saint Olaf College in Northfield, Minn., professors encouraged her to concentrate on voice studies, although she was rejected by the school's famed traveling choir because of her crutches. At 19, disaster struck again when she broke her left leg below the knee in 30 places in an auto accident. The setback only steeled her will to walk again.

In 1972 she confidently signed up for a Metropolitan Opera audition, rehearsed five arias and, feeling "well prepared and in good voice," sang her heart out. She was offered a scholarship and a chance to tour, giving recital programs with the Met's rookies, but the house had no place for a partial paraplegic in its regular performances. Gubrud ruefully concluded, "If I was ever going to sing opera with a major company, I was going to have to walk."

She moved from Manhattan to Chicago to work with John Scudder, a former aeronautical engineer who had devised a therapy program of exercise and meditation. At first "her feet were like limp flags at the end of flagpoles," he recalls. Gubrud spent three years under his care, and in last month's Opera St. Paul production of *La Bohème,* she was able to go onstage leaning on a single black crutch.

Gubrud acknowledged the encouragement of the cast (she smiled when, just before curtain time, someone wished her luck with the traditional "Break a leg!"). Looking ahead, Gubrud concluded she could be comfortable in physically undemanding roles like Desdemona in Verdi's *Otello,* but she adds, "I'm not out to prove I can do everything, just what is credible." How about the Met in New York? "I think it's possible," she says. "This much of my dream has come true. Why not the rest of it?"

August 18, 1980
December 14, 1981

The grande dame of dance stands up to a crippling stroke

BY DOLLY LANGDON

She is one of Broadway's most celebrated choreographers, a tiny, white-haired woman with ice-blue eyes and a commanding manner that some call tyrannical. At 75, Agnes de Mille is deprived of the spontaneous movement she once took for granted—her entire right side is partially paralyzed from a massive stroke six years ago—but she remains as willful, and often as terrifying, as she was in her physical prime. "Glaciers move faster than I do," she complains, yet every day she stands for 20 minutes at the practice barre in her Greenwich Village apartment, inching her limp right leg into the five positions of classical ballet and forcing her numb right arm to assume a *port de bras.* "It's no fun," she says. "I can't feel. I can't see improvement. It's not like recovering from a ski accident. I've lost half my body forever."

For de Mille, forever began May 15, 1975, two hours before she was to go on stage at Manhattan's Hunter College as narrator for her Agnes de Mille Heritage Dance Theatre. "I'd been warned I had high blood pressure, but I was just too busy to take the pills," she recalls sadly. "Then at the last minute I had to fire a dancer and hire a new one. When the new boy arrived, I went to sign his contract and the pen fell from my hand. Somebody said, 'Sit down and relax.' I did, and then I said, 'I can't feel my right foot, my right hand. I feel cold.' I realized I'd better ask for an ambulance."

De Mille spent the rest of that harrowing night in intensive care, balanced precariously between life and death. Later her doctors worked for three months to stop a series of embolisms and repaired the obstructed carotid artery in her neck with a length of plastic tubing. She left the hospital in a wheelchair, painfully aware that she could never fully recover.

"The nurse said it's as though all the telephone lines had been dragged out of a switchboard and just left on the floor," she explains. "I give the signals and nothing happens. It took me a year to learn to hold up my right hand. I control it from back in my left shoulder. It feels as if it weighs 70 pounds." Disciplined and sublimely stubborn, de Mille taught herself to write with her left hand and to walk with a cane and a leg brace. "But I am deprived of what all danc-

"I've never been a very kind person. I'm me. And I had to do what I had to do," said de Mille, surveying her career as a choreographer.

ers and choreographers have to have," she says with a sigh. "The instinctive gesture."

De Mille chose to turn her struggle into a memoir, *Reprieve*. It is her 11th book, and it will carry a twofold message. "First," she says, "that you can have a life after something like this if you really persist. Don't try to do the impossible. Just lower your sights and zero in on what you can do. Second, that you will discover a tremendous awareness of other faculties. Your capacity just opens up. It's extraordinary."

That is the word most often reserved for de Mille herself. Along with Isadora Duncan and Martha Graham, she is revered—and, by some traditionalists, deplored—for shaping the evolution of American dance in this century. Her "overnight success" in 1943 as the choreographer of *Oklahoma!*, a Broadway debut that revolutionized American musicals, followed 15 years of rejection and striving. Previously, dance in musical dramas had been all frills and decoration; de Mille believed that dance should be seamlessly integrated into plot and character. In the years that followed, she carried out her ambition on Broadway in hits like *Carousel, Paint Your Wagon* and *Brigadoon.*

De Mille got her first Broadway job as choreographer for a 1932 Shubert musical called *Flying Colors.* But she was fired before the show even opened in New York for taking too long to make up the dances. Discouraged, she took the next boat to Europe, where she studied some and worked less. With war imminent, she returned in 1938 to the U.S. stone-broke. She thereupon landed a $20-a-week job teaching dance, and had her teeth straightened—on credit.

In 1939 a wealthy dance enthusiast named Lucia Chase decided to bankroll the company that later became the American Ballet Theatre, and Agnes was signed as a choreographer. By 1942 her work had brought her to the attention of the Ballet Russe de Monte Carlo, which, for novelty's sake, had decided to include a ballet by an American in its classical repertoire. De Mille created *Rodeo* out of sketches she had done in England and demanded Aaron Copland as her composer. "If it is possible for a life to change at one given moment," she says, "my hour struck at 9:40 p.m., October 16, 1942. Chewing gum, squinting under a Texas hat, I turned to face what I had been preparing for the whole of my life." There were 22 curtain calls, and in the audience were Richard Rodgers and Oscar Hammerstein, on the verge of their hit, *Oklahoma!*

Just as her star was unexpectedly rising,

de Mille met Walter Prude, a Texas-born concert manager, and fell in love. When he was drafted into the Army, Agnes followed him from one training camp to another and married him just weeks before he was sent overseas. Two and a half years later Walter returned. In 1946 their only child, Jonathan, was born. (He is now married and a professor of history at Emory University in Atlanta.) He was desperately ill for his first five years and de Mille found herself both a working mother and a nurse. Further, her husband was outspokenly resentful of her career. Yet the marriage had saving quality, too. "Somehow," muses Agnes, "we always delighted each other."

Enough, in fact, to sustain the marriage for 38 years. "I'm a cripple now," Agnes says frankly. "I'm dependent on Walter. He's been an angel to me. He'll come home tonight and fix my dinner and sit beside me. We'll look at TV together and read and go to sleep. It's all very *gemütlich.*" Yet it would be a mistake to regard this peace as surrender. Even now, as de Mille wrestles her traitorous right leg into position, she dreams the improbable dream that she may once again make it perform. "But even if I don't," she adds with a defiant smile, "you can say I certainly used it when I had it, kiddo."

September 21, 1981

COPING

Down's syndrome is a tough foe for a U.S. Senator's family

BY LOWELL AND
CAMILLE WEICKER

The birth of a son in 1978 posed more than the usual child-rearing worries for U.S. Senator from Connecticut Lowell Weicker Jr. and his wife Camille. Their son, Sonny Davidson Weicker, was born at Georgetown University Hospital in Washington, D.C., suffering from Down's syndrome, a genetic birth defect that causes varying degrees of mental retardation, hearing and speech impairment and other physical difficulties. The parents spoke of the experience with PEOPLE's Clare Crawford-Mason.

Camille: On the way to the hospital I had a feeling something was wrong. It was June 12th and just awful out—lightning and thunder. I remember thinking I didn't want my baby born on the 13th. Lowell helped in the delivery, and we both held him as soon as he was born. He had a full face and looked just like his father.

Lowell: He was born around 2 or 3 in the morning. I left and came home, and then at 5 or 6 Camille telephoned, obviously upset.

Camille: The doctor had come in and said, "There's something wrong. We're not sure, but we think your son has a problem." Within an hour the head of the genetics department came in, and he said, "There's no sense in fooling you. It takes two or three days to do the chromosome test, but I can tell you, based on my experience, that he's Down's." "Down's? What is Down's?" "Down's syndrome," he said. "They used to call it mongolism." My brother was pre-med and when I was 8, I remember going into a laboratory. There in bottles they had mongoloid fetuses. When the doctor said "mongolism," it hit like a ton of bricks.

Lowell: It was a real kick in the tail. I suppose my first thought was, my God, what an experience for Camille.

Camille: He cried. He can say "No." But he cried.

Lowell: We were crying for ourselves, not the baby. When I got back to the hospital, Camille was sitting on the bed, tears rolling down her face. The head of genetics was there. He said, "You have several options: to leave the baby now, to think about it and then leave the baby, or to take the baby home." There were no options for me; there wasn't any debate in my mind at all.

Camille: We talked and we talked, and he turned to the doctor and said, "You know, this is the greatest fight that I've ever had, and I'm a fighter." I had seriously considered not taking the baby home. I thought by putting him in an institution I could pretend it never happened and start all over again. That lasted about five minutes. He was ours and we were responsible for him. If my husband was willing to try, then so was I.

Lowell: From that moment on there has never been a look back. Life goes on, and the job goes on.

Camille: I had a friend who once said, "Camille, if you can't manage day to day, manage hour to hour. And if you can't manage hour to hour, just take the next five minutes." The first three months of Sonny's life drove me nuts because I wasn't doing anything; I felt like my hands were tied. The doctor said, "As soon as you start classes, you'll feel a sense of accomplishment," and he was right. When Sonny was 3 months, we

Though shocked by their son's handicap, the Weickers decided, "The only way people would accept Sonny was if we did."

joined a public infant-stimulation program. The first year you're really working with motor skills. Sonny could not lift his head, and I mean we spent three months on that. The other side of the school was the mothers' meetings where I sat and cried out my problems. You feel personally responsible for your child not being normal. As a mother of a Down's child, you're always walking a tightrope. You want to push him to the fullest of his potential, but you've got to recognize where his potential is and not push too hard. I used to worry about the time he spent sleeping because he wasn't learning. We went to the doctor and he said, "Camille, he's growing; leave him alone. He needs his sleep."

Lowell: There comes a point very early on in the Down's child's life where the learning process slows down. Whatever's going to be achieved has to be achieved soon.

Camille: And Down's children can regress. This summer we were living right on the Mystic River, boats all over the place. Every day Sonny heard the word "boat" and could sing "Row, row, row your boat" with me. But now he doesn't say "boat" anymore. It's discouraging, but I get some true rewards. Sonny does achieve; he is walking, he's running, he's doing well. He comes in at 5:30 in the morning, and he pokes open my eye and says, "eye." Half of me says, "Oh, you rotten kid," for waking me up, and the other half says, "Isn't that marvelous; he can say 'eye.'"

Lowell: It's still early; they can't make a definitive evaluation until Sonny's 3 or 4 as to how far he can go. He's enrolled in a public nursery school now in suburban Virginia that is marvelous. I think he'll be right at the top of the scale of what a Down's child can do. He has more personality, more love; he's got a sense of humor; he's got everything. I'm no great expert on Down's; we've had excellent counseling as to what Sonny needs in a technical sense.

Camille: Of course, part of coping with a handicapped child is, what do you do with the rest of your life? Right now he's a baby and he's cute. There's nothing cute about a 16-year-old with a beard, sitting on a mat soiling himself. So if parents choose to institutionalize a child, I no longer judge them. I would like to think that if Sonny's development leveled off at the 6-month level I'd keep him forever, but I don't know that.

Lowell: If I were a baby-sitter, I'd rather sit with Sonny than a normal child. Down's children want to learn, to do what you do. They're not spoiled or whiny. I can sit with him for six hours and be absolutely fascinated by the way he works at everything and wants to learn everything, by the way he imitates. Even now people refer to this as a tragedy for us. It's hard to convince them otherwise, because they think we're bearing our cross with a smile. There's no coping; he's not in any way a burden. We're not bearing any damn cross.

Camille: I don't agree. There was a lot of coping. It was hard for Lowell's parents at first. But now Sonny has brought everybody in our family closer together. He brings out the best in people. Lowell and I can really argue and scream, but then we realize our main goal in this world is Sonny, and isn't it silly to waste energy arguing. My own earliest memories are of my grandmother telling me how beautiful I was. Beautiful was the word she used as every new baby came into our family, and there were many. It was not until I was well grown that I learned my grandmother was totally blind and had been since the age of 10. But beautiful was the word she used, and that was the way she saw children, with the eyes of her soul. Two and a half years ago I was a newlywed and a mother-to-be. Like every expectant mother, I had great dreams for my child. In 20 minutes, my dreams ended. I wish I could say that I accepted immediately, but I didn't. My biggest regret in looking back was having wasted those first 24 hours with grief and tears. Four months later I became pregnant again. One reason, awful as it sounds, was that I felt Sonny should have someone to grow up with and to take care of him. The odds were one in 100 of having another Down's child, so I had amniocentesis. Then I waited four horrible weeks for the results. I couldn't sleep nights. I'm Roman Catholic and I don't believe in abortion, but I don't know what I would have done. I was five months pregnant when we finally found out the good news. Now we are blessed with Lowell Palmer Weicker III. Tre, we have nicknamed him. He and Sonny get along great; they chatter for hours. But sometimes I think "Tre, darn it, it's so easy for you." Sonny didn't walk until he was 20 months; Tre just got up at 12 months and took off.

Lowell: I think Sonny's going to be able to lead an independent life. Obviously he will have to have people watching over his financial affairs, his living, but I fully expect that he's going to be able to do a job of some sort and live independently.

Camille: My dreams for Tre have changed. I don't care if he is the founder of a great pharmaceutical firm or a United States Senator. I care that he is healthy, happy and has a deep concern for his brothers, his sisters and his fellow man. I look at my two infant sons, each so beautiful. Tre, whose eyes just sparkle, and Sonny, whose eyes have a glow. And I know that each will cast a special light on this world.

December 1, 1980

Sonny, whose language and speech skills progressed, was later slated for special education classes in public school.

"We named the baby Sonny because we'd heard Down's children were sunny of disposition," said Camille. Added Dad: "I don't think of him as not being normal. He's a joy."

231

COPING

Conquering her stutter becomes a political wife's triumph

BY ANNIE GLENN

Of the two million Americans who stutter, few have faced that problem in as public a fashion as Annie Glenn. As the wife of astronaut-turned-U.S. Senator John Glenn, she gamely greeted Presidents and constituents as the occasion demanded while striving mightily to make herself seen but not heard. At 53, however, she entered a special therapy program that finally helped her overcome her speech impediment, and subsequently she described her long struggle with stuttering to PEOPLE's *Margie Bonnett. After this story appeared, Annie Glenn went on to campaign actively—and publicly—in her husband's race for the Democratic presidential nomination.*

I was considered to have an 85 percent speech impediment, which means I stuttered that much of the time. My father, a dentist, also stuttered, and so to me it seemed like a way of life. Only once can I remember being laughed at as a child because of my speech. I was reciting a poem in sixth grade; I was really crushed, but I didn't tell my parents about it. After that I was never made to get up in front of the class.

I can remember some very painful later experiences—especially the ridicule. People would tell me to hurry up or start shouting at me because they thought I was deaf and dumb. Going into a department store used to be terrifying. I would never ask where certain items were because I was afraid of being laughed at. Instead, I would hunt and hunt. When I wanted to travel, I couldn't tell the man at the ticket counter where I wanted to go. I had to write out my destination and show it to him.

Can you imagine living in the modern world and being afraid to use the telephone? "Hello" used to be so hard for me to say. I worried that my children would be injured and need a doctor. Could I somehow find the words to get the information across on the phone?

John was always very thoughtful and pa-

tient, and he never made the slightest attempt to keep me in the background. All the same, the years he was in the space program were tough. I don't think any of us was fully prepared for the press attention that followed his orbital flight. I can remember when the seven Mercury astronauts' wives were asked to be on a Bob Hope special, and each of us was given something to say. I told them at the first rehearsal that I just wouldn't be able to speak.

By then I had taken three traditional speech therapy courses, but they had been more helpful for my morale than my stutter. Then one morning at breakfast John and I saw a television interview with Ron Webster, director of the Hollins Communications Research Institute, about a new treatment for stuttering. John asked me if I'd like to try it. I said yes—and became one of the institute's first 100 students.

During the three-week course in Roanoke, Va., we worked 11 hours a day. Some doctors now believe that stuttering has physical rather than emotional causes. Dr. Webster thinks it involves a defect in a person's voice feedback. It appears as if some mechanism in the ears of the stutterer cancels out some of the information in the sound of the voice. When it doesn't get to the brain, the speech muscles jump out of control. At the institute we began by pronouncing one-syllable words like "my" and "on" very slowly, two seconds per syllable, observing how it was formed in our throat,

mouth and jaw. We also learned how to breathe; most stutterers take very shallow breaths from their chest, then get tense in their throat or jaw. The second week we sped up to one second per syllable, and by the third we were speaking at a normal rate and even making telephone calls. Finally, we went to shopping centers and practiced in public what we had learned.

A new world has opened up for me. Now I give talks for John; I can argue; I can say lengthy things I've never been able to say. I walk up to perfect strangers in the Capitol building and ask if I can help when they look lost. That's something I've never been able to do before.

I still think I've got a long way to go. But now when people are rude or impatient when I'm out in public, I say, "Wait a minute, I'm a stutterer. Just be patient." It takes a long time to gain the confidence to say that. I keep working with a speech therapist at Walter Reed Army Medical Center in Washington, and I have been back to Hollins twice. I always emphasize that this particular speech therapy works for me, but it may not work for everyone. The most important part of what's happened is that now I can get my ideas across. I used to be just a good listener; now I'm a chatterbox. John kids me that the phone bills have gone sky-high. My greatest pride is when I am able to encourage other stutterers to come out of hiding and tackle their own problem.

October 13, 1980

After overcoming her handicap, Annie joined a speakers' club for Senate wives, then later became a busy public speaker when hubby John's campaign for the Presidency took off.

Memory of a childhood rape endures to haunt a popular poet

BY ROD McKUEN

For years Rod McKuen translated his most deeply personal thoughts into immensely popular collections of poetry and song. One experience of his early life, however, long remained unspoken: his ordeal as a sexually abused child. In a painfully candid conversation with PEOPLE's Clare Crawford-Mason, the then-49-year-old writer spoke at length about the boyhood trauma he secretly carried with him into manhood. Since making these revelations, McKuen became an active member of the National Committee for the Prevention of Child Abuse, lecturing, counseling and fund-raising in its behalf.

After going public with his story of sexual abuse, McKuen began counseling abused kids in L.A. His message to would-be molesters: "If I see you on the street, you'd better run."

The fact that my stepfather had beaten me up when I was a kid wasn't hard for me to talk or write about. I had both arms broken and my ribs caved in several times, but physical injuries on the outside heal. Before now, though, I have never been able to talk about having been sexually abused when I was a child. Those scars have never healed, and I expect they never will.

My aunt, who was my stepfather's sister, was baby-sitting with me when I was 7. She began to sort of fondle me, and I said, "Don't do that. I don't like that." She said, "I love you. I'm your aunt." I said, "I know, but don't do that," and I finally started getting a little bit hysterical and started screaming. I remember it really vividly, and she stopped and left before my mother got home.

Then about two weeks later my uncle, her husband, took me on a hunting trip near Hoover Dam, and I was really looking forward to it. We got into his pickup truck, and off we went with sleeping bags and everything. I liked him a lot because he told me really good stories, and he was always fun to be with. I loved it when he'd come over to the house and hug me and carry me on his shoulders and take me for walks.

We sat by the campfire until about 10 or 11 o'clock and talked. Finally I got in my sleeping bag, and he got in his. Then he said, "Rodney"—at that time everybody called me Rodney, which I hate—"are you asleep?" I said, "No, I'm not. I don't know why." He said, "I'm not either." We were out in the wilds, and it was a little scary, because there were a lot of animals and night

sounds I was unfamiliar with. He said, "I bet you're scared." I said, "Oh, a little bit, I guess." He said, "Why don't you just come over and get in my sleeping bag?" I said, "Yes, that's probably a good idea, great." So I got into his sleeping bag and we each talked. We were very close, of course. That closeness didn't bother me at all, because this was somebody I loved and trusted.

And then things started happening. He ended up raping me. It was painful, but worse than the pain was the fact that it was happening. All the wonderful times we had had together were gone, and I kept thinking to myself, "What did I do to make him turn against me? To make him hate me so much that he would do this to me?" I had already been wondering about my aunt.

I didn't cry until I got back to my own sleeping bag. He had been satisfied and was just as glad to get rid of me. He certainly didn't want to wake up with a child whom he had sodomized. In the morning I couldn't look at him. Then I started getting really mad. I said, "Listen, your wife did something like this, too. I'm not going to tell my mother about this, but if you even look at me again, if you come near me again, if you do anything at all, I'm not only going to tell my mother, I'm going to run down the street and tell everybody on the block." Something told me this was a time for blackmail.

I only saw them a couple of times afterward, and anytime there was a danger of their names coming up, I always found a way to change the subject. But I thought about what happened almost every day until I was in my 30s. All my life I have felt that

somehow I did something, that I was asking to be touched, to be victimized, that I must have done something to bring it on. I don't know how to get rid of that feeling. It doesn't go away, mainly because you can't share it. You don't want to tell anybody because you're afraid people will think even less of you than you think of yourself.

I am sure that is why I was so confused about my sexual identity. I was frightened by sex. It wasn't until I was in my 20s that I had my first satisfactory sexual experience. Also, I've always had an inferiority complex, and that childhood incident intensified it. I think that's one of the reasons I've always worked and never taken vacations. I'm trying to be as good as everybody else.

Eventually I started to have dreams. I'd find myself getting out of that sleeping bag and going to the edge of a cliff and getting ready to jump off. I started taking sleeping pills, and I knew that people could get hooked on pills. I was in my 30s. I was sure there was something wrong with me.

Even the weeks after I first told of the rape were awful. I was on tour for the Child Abuse Committee, and each time I retold the story I felt it more vividly. I had to stop the tour and come home. Now I'm dealing with it better. I have resumed my speeches and am heading back on the concert trail. Now I am not afraid of anything or anybody.

My advice to a young person who is being sexually intimidated is to tell somebody immediately. If it's your father or mother, tell the other parent. If they don't believe you, tell your brother or sister, if you have one. If they don't believe you and you go to

233

COPING

church, tell your minister, tell anybody you trust. As a last resort, go to the police, but tell somebody. Children are warned not to accept sweets from strangers, but nobody warns little sister about Daddy. When I was growing up, incest was considered a joke, something that happened in the Appalachians. Well, it's happening next door and in the next room. It's just that nobody ever talks about it.

We need sex education in schools, but we need it at home first. We need parents to learn the names of the teachers who are teaching their children. We need families to question day-care centers, to question other children and their own as to what goes on. My advice to adults who are sexually abusing a child, or are tempted to, is to seek out help. You are taking away things from your children before they even receive them, and they may never have a feeling of self-respect or self-worth. The best prevention is for everyone who cares about the human condition to get involved. I think we all have an obligation to make children our business whether they're our own or not.

August 16, 1982

McKuen kept silent about his childhood attack for years, admitting he could not face public disclosure. "I knew that once I told," he explained, "I could never take it back."

Toxic shock changes a victim's view of life

By Roger Wolmuth

After a 1981 Thanksgiving Day dinner with her family in Rockford, Ill., New York Times reporter Nan Robertson suddenly collapsed and was rushed to a local hospital. A victim of toxic shock syndrome, the 55-year-old journalist underwent 11 weeks of medical treatment, the partial amputation of eight fingers and a painful rehabilitation at Manhattan's Rusk Institute. Robertson recalled the ordeal in the interview below with PEOPLE *Senior Writer Roger Wolmuth. Four months later she was awarded the Pulitzer Prize for her own account of the experience in the* New York Times.

What were your first symptoms of toxic shock?

Immediately after finishing my Thanksgiving dinner, I just threw up the whole meal. I attributed it to fatigue and travel and the excitement at seeing my family. That night I awakened in a kind of trance just before 3 in the morning and found myself crawling and crashing up the staircase to the bathroom on the second floor. I could feel my arms and legs becoming paralyzed, and my vomiting and diarrhea were uncontrollable. I had made a mess as I went upstairs, and my instinct was to get to the bathtub to clean myself. My brother-in-law and sister came into the bathroom and found me sitting there in my filthy nightgown, too weak to turn on the water. They carried me to the den where I could hear them talking. My sister thought it was the 24-hour flu, but my brother-in-law was alarmed. He said, "No, she has no pulse. It's serious."

Were you aware of what was going on?

I was disoriented and confused, but I could hear everything. The ambulance arrived, and they were starting to take me to Rockford Memorial, which is about a 15-minute drive across town. At a nearby intersection, I could hear the medical attendant cry out, "Left! Left! Go to St. Anthony! She has no pulse. If we go to St. Anthony, it's only three minutes, and she'll have a chance." By the time we reached this Roman Catholic hospital, my fingers and my feet were darkening with the initial stages of gangrene; the toxic shock had shut off my vascular system, and when that happens, the extremities are the first things to go. By 7:30, I had had four of the five classic symptoms of toxic shock—vomiting, diar-

234

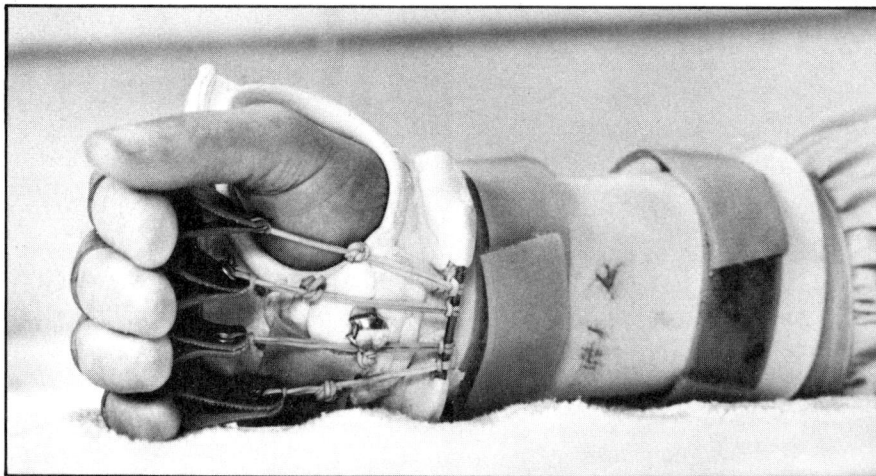

Doctors used this wrist brace to help Robertson regain flexibility in her traumatized fingers. "It was like a rubber band retainer on a teenager's teeth," explained Nan.

rhea, plummeting blood pressure and a sunburn-like rash. I later developed a fever of more than 102°, the fifth symptom.

What was the treatment?

First they flushed the toxins, which of course are poisons, out of the body. I had lost about 10 quarts of fluid in diarrhea and vomiting, and they pumped in 24 quarts of fluid filled with antibiotics to fight the *Staphylococcus aureus.* A strain of this very common bacterium is what presumably causes toxic shock. I gained 40 pounds in 24 hours and blew up like a Michelin tire man. It was grotesque. For two days I slipped into a coma, and for almost three weeks I was on a respirator so I could breathe but not speak. In all, I had 14 doctors treating me—cardiologists, lung specialists, dermatologists, internists, almost every kind of specialist you can imagine. Although my thumbs were spared, my other eight fingers turned black; they thought they'd have to amputate the right leg and toes of the left foot.

How did they save you?

They began manipulating the joints of my fingers to enable the circulation to return. The gangrene had turned into black, hard sheaths on the fingers, and the doctors, with great pain to me, would peel this dry gangrene away to the healthy flesh underneath. They used all kinds of splints and braces and exercises to make my feet and legs come back. As soon as I was well enough to stand it, they had me walking in orthopedic shoes with iron braces up to the knees. But they could not save the end joints of my fingers.

Was the amputation as bad as you thought it would be?

It was terrifying. When they came to remove the bandages two days later, I turned my head aside. I thought my hands were go-

ing to be awful looking. Finally I held them up, looked at them and rotated them back and forth. The tips were very red and covered with black surgical stitches, but I said to the doctors—with a smile—"I can live with this." The fingers were enormously sensitive, though, and 10 days later, when I finally returned to New York and entered the Rusk Institute, the stitches were still in my hands. Dr. Barry Zide, a young plastic

surgeon, who later did a second and third operation on my hands in New York, was able to throw a nerve block on my wrists, which blocked sensation to my fingers, and removed the stitches painlessly. The two subsequent operations not only made the hands look much better, but Dr. Zide put little pads of skin at the ends of my fingers so that I would be able to touch without pain.

What was it like when you got home?

I found I was helpless. My hands were stiffened and traumatized; I couldn't turn a knob or faucet or dress myself. I couldn't wash myself or even wipe myself after I went to the bathroom. I couldn't do *anything.* I had a nurse's aide during the day for about six weeks, and I got a half dozen of my women friends to rotate every night, fixing me dinner, undressing me and putting me to bed. I also had out-patient therapy at Rusk every day. I kept a diary, and on Feb. 26 I was finally able to tie a bow.

How are your hands now?

I can take notes almost as quickly as I used to, but I still can't type at my old speed. For one thing, my fingers are about an inch shorter, and the intervals on the keyboard are different. I try to use all the fingers, but

"Pain does make you tougher—if you survive it," said Robertson, who had to undergo some stressful moments during her daily therapy sessions at Manhattan's Rusk Institute.

COPING

sometimes my thoughts rush ahead of my hands, and I find myself poking with my thumbs. But my life is very normal now. I can live independently and alone.

What caused your toxic shock?

In my case, it was *not* tampons. I had not menstruated for over 11 years. Doctors believe what happened was that there was a tiny sore on my vaginal wall. The bacterium, which was probably on my skin, made its way to the vagina, fastened on this tiny sore, grew there and sent out these toxins into my body. Something that simple.

What do medical researchers find in most cases of toxic shock?

In the great majority of cases, the link between tampons and toxic shock syndrome is as convincing to me as between cigarettes and lung cancer. The larger and more absorbent the tampon, the higher the risk.

Will your life ever be the same?

Some part of me has been taken away and can never be given back. I have been through terrible pain, and I feel stronger than I was before and also more vulnerable. I have always believed in seizing the moment, and this has been enormously sharpened in me. I don't know what my life will bring, but I'm a walking miracle, and I realize it. I have not only survived; I have prevailed!

December 13, 1982

Although her doctors feared she would never walk again, Nan strutted with the best. Back at work, with a Pulitzer Prize to her credit, she exulted: "My life is a wonderful life."

EVELYN FLORET

A statesman's sudden affair of the heart cuts deep

BY HENRY KISSINGER

Joking that it proved "I do have a heart," former Secretary of State Hènry Kissinger joined an estimated 100,000 other Americans who faced bypass heart surgery in 1982. In a four-and-a-half-hour operation, doctors removed 18 inches of vein from the diplomat's right leg and used it to detour around three clogged arteries leading from his heart. Weeks later while convalescing in Palm Springs, Kissinger recalled his ordeal for PEOPLE's Gail Jennes.

I had had constant pain in my right shoulder and neck from two separate injuries for about a year and a half. At one point I went to a doctor about the shoulder and he wanted to operate, thinking it was an orthopedic problem. I was working on my book, so I didn't want to face surgery. Then last fall an acute pain developed right next to it, down my shoulder blade and across my right collarbone, so I made an appointment at Massachusetts General Hospital. They found there was something amiss orthopedically but not enough to explain the severity of the pain. The doctor suggested I return for a stess test to see if the heart was involved.

A week or two later there was a blizzard in New York. I had to abandon my car at the U.N. and walk about six blocks to my apartment. On the way, the pain became excruciating. Also, for the first time, I noticed a shortness of breath. I told this to my wife, Nancy. We were going to Acapulco, but she said she wouldn't go unless I had another checkup. She called Dr. W. Gerald Austen, an old friend and one of this country's noted heart specialists. He arranged for me to return to Mass General for two days.

They took an angiogram the morning of Feb. 8 and found that one artery was 100 percent blocked. So I only had two functioning, and one of those was 60 percent blocked. They felt I'd better get an operation as quickly as possible.

I have no way of knowing what caused my heart problem. I've never smoked; I almost never drink. I've always had the idea that I had enormous endurance. When more work needed to be done, I just added three or four hours to the day or worked through the night. Four or five hours' sleep was average. I certainly hadn't been taking care of

Kissinger convalesced in Palm Springs and credited "outstanding doctors and a basically strong constitution" for his quick recovery.

myself, and I certainly didn't watch my food intake. I didn't spend enough time on exercise. The best I ever managed was an occasional swim or walk. I suppose all these factors contributed, but I don't know.

All the doctors said that I was going to have a hellish two days after the surgery, but that I'd never remember a minute afterward. It's true I had a bad two days, but I remember it all. You come out of that operation with some 12 lines and drainage tubes connecting you to such things as the IVs, the electrocardiographic and blood pressure monitors. Because of the respirator, you have a gag down your throat and can't make a sound. It's not pleasant. As soon as I came out of anesthesia, I began writing notes to Nancy and the doctors asking when the gag would be removed and urging Nancy to go to the hotel for some sleep.

It was a new experience for me to be absolutely dependent on people. I couldn't even turn over without the nurses helping me because the pain would have been too great. Still I had to be turned regularly, and my vital signs had to be taken every half hour. So I would just doze off, and then

somebody would wake me up, give me a pill or take my pulse. All I wanted was to be left alone. They asked Nancy what music I hated most. She said rock 'n' roll, so they put on some rock 'n' roll music just to get the juices flowing again. Then they put a movie on television. I was still so doped I couldn't fully understand it. But they kept me alert through that first night.

One of the least pleasant aspects of recuperating is that they make you cough after they've broken your breastbone in order to get at your heart. They make you cough seven or eight times a day to prevent pneumonia. One person said you think the terrible time is when you cough; in fact, it's that first sneeze. Mine was no joke, but luckily it came three weeks after surgery.

I owe a lot to Nancy for getting me through the first few days of my recovery. She stayed with me the whole time, when things were the most painful. Three days after the operation I was having visitors and trying to stay as close to my normal concerns as I could.

I didn't begin to work until I left the cardiac care section eight days after surgery. I

don't want to give you the wrong impression. I was working maybe an hour a day then, not eight hours a day. Eight hours is about two-thirds of what I usually do.

I weighed more than 200 pounds at the time of the operation but have lost 19 since then and have another 15 to go. All the things I like are bad for me. I like sausage. I like whipped cream. I like lots of eggs. Lately I have been eating a lot of salads—not my favorite—and chicken. Still, I can't do better than lose three or four pounds a week. But I have to keep it off. I don't want to go through this again.

There is no question that when you learn that you have physical limits, that is something important in your life to think about. But although surgery was a painful experience, there is not going to be a traumatic change in my life. I return to Mass General on April 16 for a postoperative checkup. The day before, I am going to take all the doctors on my case and their wives, 17 people, to dinner at Locke-Ober—and I will break their hearts by breaking my training in the most egregious fashion.

April 5, 1982

237

COPING

Pat Boone's daughter Cherry fights back from anorexia

BY BILL SHAW

They'd had something of a scene. Finally Cherry Boone promised her fiancé, Dan O'Neill, that she would never again gorge herself with food only to throw it up. Dan took her at her word—after all, if you couldn't trust Pat Boone's eldest daughter, whom could you trust? As he drove off into the night, Cherry walked into the family's Beverly Hills home and stared at the meat scraps left for her dog, Summa. Minutes later, returning unannounced to the house, Dan remembers witnessing the most "revolting and pathetic thing I'd ever seen." His wife-to-be was sitting on the kitchen floor, eating out of the dog's dish. "I nearly broke off the engagement," he remembers. "But I realized she must be sick, and I loved her enough that I

During the worst phase of her anorexia in 1975 (above), 21-year-old Cherry weighed in at a scant 88 pounds.

wanted to help her if I could."

Dan, now 34, and Cherry, 28, were married in 1975 as planned. But as she recounted in her book, *Starving for Attention* (Continuum, $12.95), it took Dan two difficult years to get Cherry the help she needed in her struggle with anorexia nervosa and bulimia, emotional eating disorders that affect nearly 100,000 young women each year.

The eldest of the four Boone girls, Cherry had started performing with her father at age 5 and at 16 was a regular on the family's stage and TV appearances. She was a natural beauty, a straight-A student at Westlake School for Girls in L.A.'s Holmby

Hills, seemingly a model member of America's model family. Yet she was also subtly burdened by being Pat Boone's daughter. "He's a good father," says Cherry. "But it was the way people responded to him and the expectations they had of his children that got to me." On TV her 140 pounds on a 5'7" frame struck her as hefty, as an unsightly blemish on her father's image. "I thought my father was perfect in every way," Cherry acknowledges, "so I wanted to be perfect too."

It was to "perfect" herself that she started dieting and exercising. When her parents and friends praised her new sleekness, she quit eating altogether. In her disturbed mind, as she sees it now, starving herself not only gained her attention and won praise for her father, but it also gave her a feeling of power. "I was controlling a part of my life," says Cherry, "a life which was controlled for the most part by other people."

It wasn't until she was 17 and weighed a mere 92 pounds that Pat and Shirley Boone realized there was something seriously wrong with their daughter. They insisted that she eat.

Cherry responded with a life full of lies. She would gorge only to vomit. She shoplifted laxatives because she was ashamed to be seen buying quantities of them. She became addicted to diet pills—with the result that at age 18 she weighed 80 pounds and found herself lying near death in an L.A. hospital. Her parents subsequently spent thousands of dollars on doctors and institutions to fatten her up—all to no avail. "You can't beat anorexia by forcing someone to eat," says Cherry. "They will just throw it up. You have to treat the reasons why someone became anorectic in the first place."

Finally, in 1977, Dan O'Neill prevailed. Some six months after she had started psychiatric treatment, Dr. Raymond E. Vath of Seattle had coaxed Cherry to come to grips with her feelings about herself. After seven years of near starvation, she began to eat properly.

Today she weighs 110 pounds and consumes 2,000 calories a day. "I eat a lot of nuts and raisins," she says, "and I have a passion for guacamole and fried tortillas." No longer interested in showbiz, she exercises moderately, attends Mass (she and Dan converted to Roman Catholicism), addresses civic groups about anorexia, and cares for her 1-year-old daughter, Brittany.

Both Cherry and Dan, executive director of Mercy Corps International, a refugee-relief agency, insist that their ordeal has brought them closer to the Boones. "My relationship with my parents is healthier than before because I'm my own person," says Cherry. "My identity no longer rises and falls with the Pat Boone family."

October 11, 1982

Cherry, who recounted her struggle for survival in a memoir titled *Starving for Attention*, credited husband Dan with helping her find the psychiatric help she desperately needed.

A Kennedy shows his own profile in courage

BY TED KENNEDY JR.

Neither family wealth nor a famous genealogy could protect Teddy Kennedy Jr. from cancer in 1973. While in seventh grade, the elder son of Ted and Joan Kennedy lost part of his right leg to surgery and underwent a grueling period of chemotherapy. Young Teddy recalled those frightening days for PEOPLE's Gail Jennes. He later graduated from Wesleyan University and planned a career in public service.

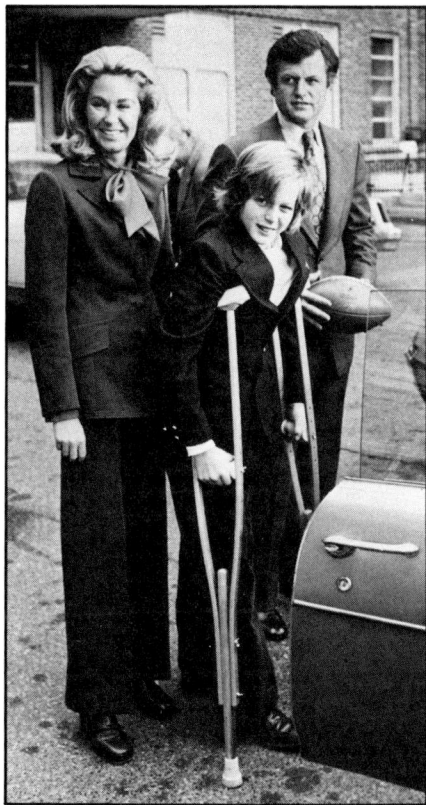

Although they later divorced (in 1983), Joan and Ted Sr. united in helping their son after his release from the hospital.

I can remember I was playing football with the team, and when I injured my leg, it hurt for an abnormal period of time. I was the first one to take the initiative to go to the doctor. I went to the pediatrician whom I'd been going to for years, and he told me to put warm packs on it and come back in two weeks or so. I finally went to Georgetown University Hospital for a diagnosis. That's where they told me they'd have to remove part of my leg.

I said, "What part? Are you going to have to remove some of the muscle here, or what are you going to have to do?" They said, "Well, no. From the knee down." That's when I realized I was going to lose my leg.

I had the operation the next day, and the day after, I was down in physical therapy learning how to use an artificial leg. So I wasted no time at all. They had put a plaster thing where my leg had been, and I got up and started walking with the help of parallel bars. I exercised in physical therapy every day at first, then I moved back home and did my studies there and went to the hospital on weekends every three weeks.

I became a guinea pig because the dosages of the drug [methotrexate] I was given were experimental at the time. The chemotherapy treatments lasted about 16 months, and they were gruesome. You lose all your hair; you vomit for about four days straight; you can't keep anything down. You lose weight, and you feel just terrible. I got to the point where even before they plugged me with needles, I started to get sick just from knowing that I would in about another hour and a half. Then they pump you up with all these drugs that make you totally oblivious to everything that's going on. That's a very tough point; you feel like you just want to run away and never go back to the hospital. Your thought is, "I don't care. I'm just not going to do this anymore. Why don't they just leave me to die?"

Usually chemotherapy involves a two- or three-year period, and after about the third month patients have had the treatment about four times. They can't imagine having to go through it 50 more times. You have to tell them that life is really worth living. I had my parents, family and close friends who were able to help me get through it. They gave me constant support which made it much, much easier.

I had my operation in November and used a cane for the first couple of months. As soon as I got my stitches out, I started to go swimming, and I began skiing that March. I learned scuba diving the summer I worked on a boat in the Mediterranean, that and waterskiing. A very funny sight—I've got a style all my own. I've tried ice skating and roller skating, which is a little more difficult. But how the hell are you going to do it unless you get out there and try? I fell about 50 times trying to get around the rink once on roller skates, but the more you do it, the better you get.

Prostheses really aren't that bad. I'm lucky because I don't have sensitive scar tissue; friends of mine who've been in motorcycle accidents are all scarred up, and it can be tender and much more difficult for them. Wearing my prosthesis during the summer gets difficult sometimes because you get hot and sweaty, and then it gets painful to walk. Where I live, I go out in shorts. There are people who have never

"I can't run, but I can do about everything else," boasted Ted Jr. who proved his point during this 1981 outing on the slopes.

seen anybody with an artificial leg walking down the street before, but in a sense I think it's good for them to see it. People walk around all over the place with artificial limbs, and you never notice it because they walk so well.

Everybody adapts to their own life and experience, and I've adapted in my own way. In my case, God has been very good, and He's been very bad. He's been good in providing me with a family and a home and a lot of luxuries that a lot of people aren't able to live with. At the same time, He's also inflicted tragedies, and the loss of my leg. But I really am not that special. There are thousands of kids lying right now in hospital rooms around this country, and they don't get any recognition at all.

I may have lost a leg, but I think that I've gained a lot of other things in the meanwhile. Maybe if you lose a leg, you can gain some heart. The great lesson I have learned from my family is that no matter how terrible things might appear at one point or another, there is a clearing in the future.

Another important lesson that I've learned is always to try your hardest, never to be a quitter. A lot of people have problems in the world, and everybody always thinks that theirs are the biggest. I think that there are two types of problems, those you should worry about and ones you shouldn't worry about. Once you find the difference, you find that most things really aren't worth worrying about.

April 27, 1981

TRIBUTE

JOHN LENNON
1940-1980

And then Yoko came home, ending a four-hour workday. John treated her like a guest, fixing her herbal tea, giving her a bit of cake, asking how her day had gone. Taking her hand, he said emphatically, "Everything I know Yoko taught me. She is my wife, my lover, my friend. People who are skeptical of our relationship are jealous."

He had become a househusband to build a closer bond with Yoko and Sean, now 5, while she had taken over his portfolio, by some estimates worth more than $200 million, and, she said, it worked for both of them. "I have learned that I have strength, too. Most important is that we both work for the family now."

After dinner John gave his son a bath and read him to sleep, then got ready to go to the studio with Yoko to put finishing touches on their album. When we reached the first floor, he looked out the window and saw a crowd. "I've had enough of screaming fans," he said. "Let's try something." He led us through a door and down a creaky, narrow staircase. Finally we were in the bowels of the Dakota, this grand and ancient building. "Ahh, we're safe," John sighed, but as we slipped out to the alley, girls appeared from nowhere to ask him when he would agree to a Beatles reunion. "When are you going back to high school?" he barked, then felt badly about it. "It's not that I don't like people," he explained. "I enjoy them. It's that it gets wearing. The postman wants an autograph. The waitress wants a handshake. Everyone wants a piece of you. It's never ending." He and Yoko got into their limo. Then he was gone.
DAVID SHEFF
December 22, 1980

RON GALELLA

ELVIS PRESLEY
1935-1977

On the streets of Memphis, vendors are hawking copies of Elvis' last will and testament for $4. In Columbus, Ga., parts of a 1956 Cadillac Eldorado that Presley once owned are being melted down into $4.95 pendants. A shirt he wore in concert sells for $500. Around the country, 100 or so Elvis imitators are putting on eerie shows—complete with drum rolls from *2001*, sweaty scarves tossed to screaming women, bodyguards, sneers and bathos. "Elvis is leading God's choir," says imitator Alan Meyer in Las Vegas, "because he's the only one great enough to do it." At least 12 tribute records have been cut, and a book by three former bodyguards, *Elvis: What Happened?*, received the biggest single copy order in history—two million from K mart. Pilgrims to Memphis still line up daily to receive flowers handed out by guards at Forest Hills mausoleum, where Elvis and his mother lie despite Vernon Presley's stated desire to move them to Graceland. "It's an odd form of reverence they have for him," says a Memphis woman who witnessed parents holding children over Graceland's walls to tear off tree limbs as souvenirs.

October 10, 1977

ELVIS
AARON
PRESLEY

JANUARY 8, 1935
AUGUST 16, 1977

VERNON ELVIS PRESLEY
GLADYS LOVE PRESLEY
LISA MARIE PRESLEY

COR VERMEULE
THE NETHERLANDS
BREDA

TRIBUTE

ANWAR SADAT
1918-1981

Sadat was an easy man to love but not to understand, a complex of enigmas. He may well have sensed that his death was at hand; his wife, Jihan, has credited him with an infallible sense of omen, and as he and his generals lined up for a formal portrait just before the parade last week, his face was tense, wary. Yet fear never informed his actions: faith did. "God to me is everything that I cherish," he said last year, as we flew over his native village. "The trees, the open horizon, the wheat that we had toiled so hard to plant...I was brought up here with values, traditions and principles. And here on this land I learned something very important, that if I am true to myself and God, I am the strongest man in the world."

MIRA AVRECH
October 19, 1981

TENNESSEE WILLIAMS

1911-1983

"I was committed to a snake pit. To come down from speed, I had to take powerful medication. It induced the most marvelous hypnosis. I would see Our Lady next to my bed. She would occupy a rocker and I would drift off to sleep with her rocking. Now one cannot pretend that one still has all the energy of youth. I certainly don't. I don't look forward to the 1980s. My mother died at the age of 94. My grandfather was a month short of 98. But they were not writers. It makes a difference."
SCOT HALLER
March 16, 1983

HENRY FONDA

1905-1982

"That's what's so scary about him—nothing seems to faze him," Jane Fonda says. "He arrives on time and knows his lines. He sits and waits like an empty vessel and when they need him he fills up, does his thing and sits down...I'm 44 years old and still he can reduce me to feeling abject helplessness." Do they communicate better since making *On Golden Pond* together? "Dad is not a communicative person, he just isn't," she says. "In the last act of life one doesn't change. I won't. And one is wrong to expect it of a parent." His virtues now, she says, are what they have always been: "He has integrity, simplicity and disdain of extreme consumption. Like Thoreau, my father plays it close to the bone."
LOIS ARMSTRONG
April 12, 1982

ARTHUR RUBINSTEIN
1887-1982

Years seemed to fall away as he struck the keys, throwing himself into Beethoven's Fifth Concerto, grimacing, boyishly punching the air with his fists, chattering in Polish. "Every time I play, it's the first time," he said. At the end visitors crowded around and later, outside his dressing room, a pack of young women pursued him to his car, applauding all the way. Rubinstein blew kisses. "When I was young," he said, "I used to have successes with women because I was young. Now I have successes with women because I am old. Middle age was the hard part."

RUDI CHELMINSKI
June 30, 1975

TRIBUTE

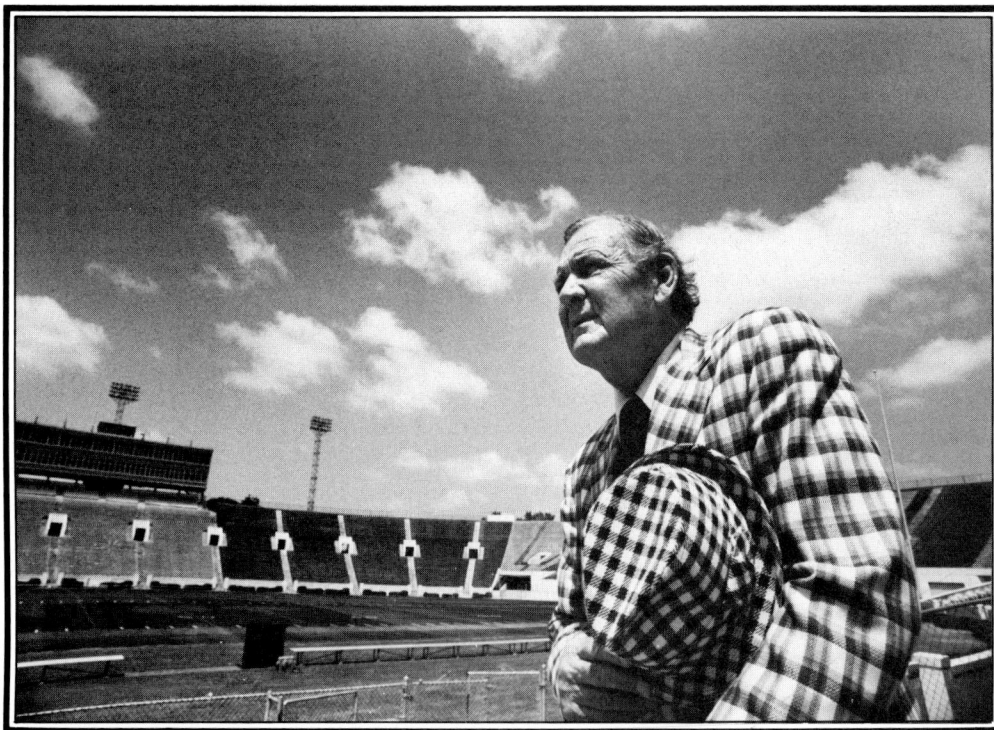

BEAR BRYANT
1913-1983

"In my lifetime, I may have put too much emphasis on winning," muses "Bear" Bryant, "because here I am an old man and the only fun I've *had* is winning, and that's ridiculous. In 30 minutes it's over and I'm looking forward to the next game. Most of the coaches who've retired tell me it's awful hard to find something to do. And the fans, well, they forget you fast. I don't know what I would do if I couldn't coach. Probably croak."

MITCHELL J. SHIELDS
October 1, 1979

KAREN CARPENTER
1950-1983

Tom Burris, the real estate developer from whom Karen was separated in 1982, says she was suffering from anorexia "for about nine years." In 1975, Karen had slipped frighteningly to a shadowy 90 pounds. It took two months of bed rest to recuperate from exhaustion after touring some 250 days a year. "It was sickening," she said. "Suddenly it wasn't fun anymore." But, clearly, Karen Carpenter intended to conquer despair. "I have," she told Dionne Warwick just two weeks before her death, "a lot of living left to do."

February 21, 1983

GRACE KELLY
1929-1982

The role of royalty seemed tailor-made for her, and she excelled in it for more than a quarter-century. At her glittering parties, while her husband usually sat and chatted with cronies, Grace would circulate among the tables, concerned that no guest feel overlooked. She was never idle. When able to relax, she loved to stitch needlepoint or arrange dried flowers, humming happily to herself. "I certainly don't think of my life as a fairy tale," she said. "I think of myself as a modern, contemporary woman who has had to deal with all kinds of problems that many women today have to deal with. I am still coping—trying to cope." Too busy to make detailed agendas for the future, she was optimistic about aging grace-fully. "No one likes the idea of getting older," she said. "It's a question of facing the inevitable and not getting upset about it. I don't plan much."

FRED HAUPTFUHRER
September 27, 1982

FREDDIE PRINZE
1954-1977

His ladies include Kitty Bruce, only daughter of the late Lenny. "She said," Freddie recalls, "that I was the first comic to make her laugh since her father. That was sweet. But the only comparison I want to Lenny Bruce is that I'm funny. I'm Freddie Prinze, Puerto Rican all the way. A lot of my old friends have been in and out of jails. They're stuck on 157th Street. One day I'd like some kid to say, 'Hey, I could be a dealer or a junkie, but, hey, screw it. Prinze got out; I'll get out.'"

S. J. DIAMOND
October 16, 1974

NATALIE WOOD
1938-1981

"I hope you guys never divorce," I told her once. "I'd stop believing in the institution of marriage if you did." "No chance," she said. "I'm not about to let him go again." She liked to describe the interlude between her first and second marriage to R.J. Wagner as a *Seitensprung.* That is a charming German expression for when two people dance, then make a little side step and swirl about the room with new partners before reuniting to finish the waltz. "You're only allowed one *Seitensprung,*" she said.

THOMAS THOMPSON
December 14, 1981

TRIBUTE

JOHN BELUSHI
1949-1982

Several years ago, Belushi was clowning with Doug Kenney, the *National Lampoon*'s co-founder, and Belushi did an impromptu impression of Elvis Presley in his death throes. Kenney told him it wasn't funny. "But," Belushi replied, "that's the way we're all going to die, Dougie." Still John Belushi didn't die without a legacy. In Chicago that night, Belushi's 27-year-old brother, Jim, starred in a road production of *The Pirates of Penzance*. After the show, he stood glassy-eyed in the lobby. "John was a genius as a comic," he said. "He gave me some advice once: When I got angry, he said, 'Go out onstage like a bull in a bull ring.'"And then Jim Belushi walked out to his limousine, mugging all the way.

March 22, 1982

SEQUEL

MIA FARROW

She was an unlikely cover girl in many ways, a saucer-eyed, sparrow-thin actress who once likened her bony frame to "an elephant's graveyard." When Mia Farrow, then 29, appeared on PEOPLE's first cover a decade ago, she evoked none of the broad-shouldered brass or buxom glamour of an earlier Hollywood. Freckled and of delicate mien, she seemed a star uncommon as the new magazine she graced.

The reason for Farrow's cover, of course, was her appearance as Daisy Buchanan opposite Robert Redford in *The Great Gatsby*, a role the supposedly fragile Farrow had wrested from both Faye Dunaway and Candice Bergen. The film, however, turned out to be only one of the productions involving Mia; midway through its shooting she announced her second pregnancy by London Symphony Conductor André Previn. Careful costuming and a quickened production schedule hid her condition from the cameras, and just one month after Mia's *Gatsby* cover story PEOPLE reported Fletcher Previn's birth.

Mixing film and family affairs was something Farrow learned early. The third of seven children born to actress Maureen O'Sullivan (who played Jane to Johnny Weissmuller's Tarzan) and director John Farrow, Mia became a star at 18, appearing as Allison MacKenzie on TV's *Peyton Place*. Very quickly her personal life began to rival any soap opera, and by 23 she had been wooed, wed and divorced from crooner Frank Sinatra, 30 years her senior. ("The secret of her appeal to men," confided mother Maureen, "is that she arouses their protective instinct.") Next, after a movie triumph in *Rosemary's Baby*, Farrow found new love with André, then 40 and married to singer-songwriter Dory Previn. The 24-year-old actress conceived twins before the conductor's divorce from Dory was granted, and Mia achieved musical notoriety in a poignant lament penned by her spurned rival. Its title: *Beware of Young Girls*.

André and Mia eventually became parents to six children (three were adopted), and with motherhood Mia's film career slowed. She starred in a 1976 TV production of *Peter Pan* and an occasional movie (*Death on the Nile*, *A Wedding*) but insisted that "stardom is full of crap" and noted that "I don't go to the premieres or wear the mink coats. I like a different kind of life." Then in 1979, after eight years of marriage, Farrow and Previn split. Returning to New York, she made a highly successful stage debut on Broadway and began arranging to take in yet another child, this time a physically handicapped Korean. "I'd like to go on and adopt more," she said recently, "I feel especially strong at this point in my life."

And so she remains. With Woody Allen as a new leading man in her off-camera life, the gamine-like actress has shown the sort of enduring appeal any screen beauty would envy. Movie audiences watching her return to the screen as a prissy woman psychiatrist in Allen's 1983 film, *Zelig*, seemed to agree. If Mia's appearance on our first cover is now but a small piece of her history, clearly that history, like our own, is still unfolding.

Gatsby done, new-mama Mia retreated to Martha's Vineyard in 1974.

ALFRED EISENSTAEDT

252

SAY CHEESE

Woody Allen and Mia make
the scene week in and
week out at Manhattan's
trendy Elaine's—so why
the coverup?

INDEX